Wittgenstein's

Philosophical Investigations

SUNY series in
Philosophy

George R. Lucas Jr., editor

WITTGENSTEIN'S PHILOSOPHICAL INVESTIGATIONS

WILLIAM H. BRENNER

STATE UNIVERSITY OF NEW YORK PRESS

Published by
State University of New York Press, Albany

Printed in the United States of America

For information, address State University of New York Press,
State University Plaza, Albany, NY 12246

Production by Laurie Searl
Marketing by Anne M. Valentine

Library of Congress Cataloging-in-Publication Data

Brenner, William H., 1941–
    Wittgenstein's philosophical investigations / William H. Brenner.
        p.   cm. — (SUNY Series in philosophy)
    Includes bibliographical references and index.
    ISBN 0–7914–4201–2 (hc. : alk. paper). — ISBN 0–7914–4202–0 (pbk.
: alk. paper)
        1. Wittgenstein, Ludwig, 1889–1951.   Philosophische
    Untersuchungen.   2. Language and languages—Philosophy.
    3. Philosophy.   I. Title.   II. Series.
B3376.W563P532355   1999
192—dc21
                                                              98–38226
                                                              CIP

10 9 8 7 6 5 4 3 2 1

To My Parents

In Grateful Memory

Philosophy is a battle against the bewitchment of

our intelligence by means of language.

My way of philosophizing . . . . consists essentially in leaving

the question of *truth* and asking about *sense* instead.

—Ludwig Wittgenstein

Contents

Preface

Among the most original thinkers of the twentieth century, Ludwig Wittgenstein has remained one of the least accessible. In this book I seek to demonstrate the essential intelligibility of his writings, the continuing freshness of his ideas, and the power of his methods.

The heart of my book is a study of selected sections of the chief work of his later period, the *Philosophical Investigations*. Presented as "a companion to the *Investigations*," its aim is to assist prospective readers find their way around the "forest of remarks" that make up this unique classic. Although I cover quite a lot of ground, I make no attempt at completeness. ("Going through the *Investigations* from cover to cover" is for *after* the sort of preliminary "field trips" described here.)

The study is preceded by an introductory essay relating Wittgenstein's ideas and methods to Parmenides, Aristotle, and other formative figures in the history of Western philosophy. It is followed by a set of essays that further develop a major theme of the *Investigations*: that there are *various* kinds of language use ("grammar")—a variety philosophy needs to look at but tends to overlook.

"Sensations, Beetles, and 'Private Language'" is a brief and (I hope) incisive interpretation of the much-discussed "private language" argument. "The Soulless Tribe" draws on Wittgenstein's last writings to clarify and deepen what he had said in the *Investigations* about "the inner life."

Colors, numbers, and the grammatical analogies between them exerted a continuing fascination on Wittgenstein; the chapters on arithmetic and color are meant to bring out the logico-philosophical depth of that fascination.

The sections headed "God" organize and develop some of Wittgenstein's fragmentary remarks on religion, theology, and ethics.

In the concluding chapter I return to the Parmenidean origins of philosophy, and to Wittgenstein's conception of its nature and limits.

The picture on the cover is of Theseus forcing the marauder Procrustes into the same iron bed he had so nefariously used on the passing travellers he robbed. I think of Wittgenstein as a philosophical Theseus doing battle against metaphysical marauders who force all varieties of language (and life) into the procrustean bed of what he calls "the model of object and designation."

Acknowledgments

Without following them in every detail, the writings of Oswald Hanfling and of Cora Diamond have been particularly important in forming my understanding of Wittgenstein. I am also indebted to Professor Diamond for a wonderfully careful critique of an earlier version of this book.

The introductory chapter and parts of chapter 5 are based on material from chapter VIII of a book I published with the University of Notre Dame Press in 1993. The chapters on "the soulless tribe," color, and theology[1] are revised versions of articles published in *The Southern Journal of Philosophy*, Nancy Simco, editor. "Arithmetic as Grammar" is a revised, augmented version of an article that appeared in a journal edited by D.Z. Phillips, *Philosophical Investigations*. I am thankful to the editors and publishers for their kind cooperation. Thanks also to: Wittgenstein's literary executors and Basil Blackwell, Ltd. for permission to quote extensively from the *Philosophical Investigations*; Alice Ambrose Lazerowitz for permission to quote extensively from *Wittgenstein's Lectures: Cambridge, 1932–35;*[2] and Cora Diamond for permission to quote extensively from *Wittgenstein's Lectures on the Foundations of Mathematics: Cambridge, 1939.*[3]

Ken Daley of the Old Dominion University Art Department drew the image used on the front cover, for which I am most grateful. It is based on a detail from a piece of Greek pottery depicting the labors of Theseus.

The five anonymous readers for the State University of New York Press made useful comments on my manuscript, as did Curtis Brooks and Duncan Richter. I thank them for their help—and apologize to those whose help I have forgotten to acknowledge.

I have tried to write in such a way that any thoughtful reader will find what I say intelligible and illuminating. Where I have succeeded, much of the credit belongs to the editorial advice of my wife Mary.

---

1. The theology article also contains an early version of the first few pages of chapter 2.

2. Edited from her own lecture notes and those of Margaret Macdonald.

3. From the notes of R.G. Bosanquet, Norman Malcolm, Rush Rhees, and Yorick Smythies.

Abbreviations

Full references are under "Wittgenstein" in the bibliography.

BB	Blue and Brown Books
CV	Culture and Value
LC	Lectures and Conversations on Aesthetics, Psychology, and Religious Belief
LFM	Lectures on the Foundations of Mathematics: Cambridge 1939
LW I	Last Writings on the Philosophy of Psychology, Vol. I
LW II	Last Writings on the Philosophy of Psychology, Vol. II
NB	Notebooks: 1914–16
OC	On Certainty
PI	Philosophical Investigations
PO	Philosophical Occasions
PG	Philosophical Grammar
PR	Philosophical Remarks
RC	Remarks on Color
RFM	Remarks on the Foundations of Mathematics
RPP I	Remarks on the Philosophy of Psychology, Vol. I
RPP II	Remarks on the Philosophy of Psychology, Vol. II
TLP	Tractatus Logico-Philosophicus
WLA	Wittgenstein's Lectures: Cambridge 1932–35 (Ambrose, ed.)
WLL	Wittgenstein's Lectures: Cambridge 1930–32 (Lee, ed.)
WLG	Wittgenstein's Lectures on Philosophical Psychology:1946–47 (Geach, ed.)
WVC	Wittgenstein and the Vienna Circle
Z	Zettel

CHAPTER ONE

Introduction

[W]e are still occupied with the same philosophical problems as were the Greeks.... because our language has remained the same and keeps seducing us into asking the same questions.

—*Culture and Value*, p. 15

THALES TO WITTGENSTEIN

Becoming

The ancient Greeks worked out many of the fundamental concepts of our civilization, including the concept of reality as a single dynamic system. The earliest of them agreed among themselves about the existence of this "system" but differed about how to describe it. While Thales said that the principle of all things is water, his successor Anaximander argued that it could be neither water nor any definite substance. Thales and Anaximander flourished in the early sixth century B.C.; later in the same century, Heraclitus spoke of reality as an "everlasting fire, kindling in measures and going out in measures" (Fragment 30). He, like his predecessors, saw unity amidst change as the essence of things; his distinctive contribution was the idea that change implies a unity of opposites ("The path up and down is one and the same" [*Fragment* 60]).

Early in the fifth century B.C. Parmenides of Elea challenged the fundamental assumption of "natural philosophers" from Thales to Heraclitus, arguing that reality is changeless and homogeneous (a "well-rounded sphere"), rather than a dynamic unity of opposites. He, like his famous pupil Zeno, regarded "motion" and every other term for change as names devoid of meaning. Why devoid of meaning? Parmenides' line of thought comes out most clearly in his argument against the sort of change called "coming into being":

1

> That which can be spoken of and thought needs must be [that is, exist] . . . (Fragment 6, in part)
>
> How can what does not exist come into existence? For if it came into existence, then earlier it was nothingness. And nothingness is unthinkable and unreal. (Fragment 8, in part)

In other words (and with added interpretation):

> Whenever we think of something, we must think of it as existing. (To think is to *picture*; to picture something is to picture it as existing.)
>
> If it makes sense to say that something will come into existence, then it makes sense to say that it does not (now) exist.
>
> If it makes sense to say that it does not exist, then it must be possible to think of it as not existing. That is not possible, however, because (to return to the first point) whenever we think of something, we must think of it as existing.

A number of philosophical theories were generated in response to Parmenides' perplexing arguments—notably, the "atomism" of Democritus, the "two worlds theory" of Plato, and the "seeds theory" of Anaxagoras. The last is relatively easy to explain. "Composite things contain the seeds of everything," according to this fifth-century philosopher. "For how could hair come from what is not hair, or flesh from what is not flesh?"[1] This "solves" the problem of how hair (for example) comes into being by saying that it didn't, really—it was there all along, hidden under other things! To "explain" something (here: coming into being) by explaining it away, as Anaxagoras seems to be doing, is an example of what we now call "reductionism." (Other examples of reductionism would be Zeno's analysis of the moving arrow into a series of discrete states—as if only what is captured in a set of "still shots" could be real, and [much later] St. Augustine's analysis of time into the threefold "present" of memory, contemplation, and expectation—as if time were a psychological phenomenon. While Zeno reduced the dynamic to the static, Augustine reduced the objective to the psychological.)[2]

Responding to the provocative arguments of his predecessors, Aristotle appears to have been the first to articulate a thoroughly nonreductive account of change. Looking at what is involved in everyday talk about coming into being, he saw that it presupposes a number of concepts—including not only

---

1. From Philip Wheelwright, ed., *The Presocratics*, p. 160.

2. Rejection of reductionism in philosophy does not imply rejection of scientific developments such as the reduction of Mendelian to molecular genetics. Zeno-like analyses of motion explain away motion; molecular theory in genetics does not explain away its Mendelian starting point.

opposites, as Heraclitus had emphasized, but also *potentiality*. The air of para-dox Parmenides sensed in "What is *not* an oak becomes an oak" (and similar statements) dissipates once we recall that what-is-not-an-oak is an acorn, that is, something potentially, but not yet actually, an oak tree. It is not that the oak comes from what is absolutely nothing, or absolutely non-oak: it comes from what is actually acorn and potentially oak. The reality of an acorn, like the reality ("being") of other natural things, goes beyond its present actuality. "That which goes beyond present actuality"—potentiality—is no thing (no object, no present actuality), but it is not absolute nothingness (pure non-being) either.

In comparing reality to "a well-rounded sphere" enclosed within itself, Parmenides was (in effect) equating it with "present actuality." In Parmenidean philosophy:

$$being = being\ there$$
$$to\ be = to\ be\ complete.$$

In Aristotelian philosophy (and common speech): "to be" is not only "to be actually such and such" but also "to be potentially so and so"; "to be" is to be in some respects incomplete, as well as in other respects "well rounded."[3]

Time and the Mind

Viewed in a philosophical spirit, everyday matters—change, time, knowledge, etc.—are objects of wonder. But when we proceed to reflect on these matters and theorize about them, we are often led into misunderstanding and paradox. And then we need to investigate the everyday, prereflective use of the words in which our reflections are expressed. What tends to block such an investigation is the same as what creates the need for it in the first place: the mind's fixing on a single, narrow case and making it the model for everything else. As the Presocratic Parmenides fixed on the "present actual-

---

3. In Aristotelian physics, natural things strive to actualize their potentialities. That may sound like an instance of the mind's tendency to project itself onto inanimate nature. But Aristotle does not speak, absurdly, of acorns consciously striving to become oaks; he speaks of nature as "unconscious art." Rather than dismissing this way of speaking as error, it would be better to characterize it as a secondary use of terms that in everyday speech are applied primarily to human and animal activities. This secondary use is Aristotle's way of expressing a certain perspective on nature as a whole—one not to be dismissed as erroneous just because it is at odds with the view of nature constructed by modern "scientific" philosophers. That it *has* been so dismissed may be an expression of the scientism permeating our civilization. Compare Wittgenstein, CV, pp. 60 j, 37 c.

ity" model of being, so the pre-medieval Augustine, and the early modern Descartes fixed on a similar model of knowing.

What is time? Augustine's meditations led him to conclude that it is something mysterious and paradoxical. He reasoned that, whatever it is, it must be something measurable. But what is there to measure—given that the past no longer exists, the future is yet to come, and the present ("the now") is just a point without extension? Wittgenstein suggests that this problem arose from making something like "measuring the length of a stick" the model for all measurement.[4] The stick is something there in front of us that we can point to and lay a ruler against. Time and its measurement can seem very mysterious when compared with a stick and its measurement.

What is mind? Is there an essential I designated by "*I*" in "I think"?[5] Picturing the I as an etherial substance perceptible to me but not others (as Descartes taught modern philosophers to do), throws little light on the actual use of the personal pronoun *I*. But it does generate skeptical problems, notably: "How can I possibly know anything about others' feelings, or they about mine? I *feel* my pains, so I *know* when I have them. Others, it seems, can only guess." Wittgenstein suggests that what lies behind this "other minds problem" (as philosophers call it) is fixation on a primitive, "object-designation" model of knowledge: "I can't point to (designate) your pains; therefore, I can't possibly know that you have what I do when I say 'pain.'"[6]

Greek mythology tells of a bandit-innkeeper by the name of *Procrustes*. When guests arrive who do not fit neatly into the uniform iron beds he provides for them, he stretches or prunes them so as to *make* them fit—killing them in the process. A mark of wisdom in philosophy is knowing how to recognize and resist "procrustean" uses of the models and ideals of the theorizing mind.

Logic and Philosophy

Philosophy is the formulation and rational defense of "world views." It began, in that sense, when Thales and Anaximander depicted the universe as an intrinsically intelligible dynamic system—rather than as the playground of

---

4. Wittgenstein makes this point in *BB*, p. 26.

5. See *BB*, pp. 66–74. I discuss these important pages in my *Logic and Philosophy*, pp. 127–130.

6. George Berkeley is usually credited with fathering "the other minds problem." But if Berkeley is its father, Descartes is its grandfather. (See *Meditations* II, particularly the passage near the end where he speaks of looking out his window at passersby and wondering if their hats and clothes might conceal automata.) I would call nearly all characteristically "modern" problems of philosophy *Cartesian*.

capricious forces depicted in Homer and Hesiod. Philosophy is also the investigation of fundamental concepts. It began, in that sense, with Parmenides' scrutiny of key terms in his predecessors' descriptions of the universe, and with Socrates' probing questions about basic moral concepts.

Aristotle was struck by the fact that his predecessors had not merely expressed opinions but also reasoned about them. This moved him to develop a system of techniques for the analysis of reasoning; he is called "the father of logic" because he was the first to develop such a system.

A "pathology of reasoning" or doctrine of fallacies was part of Aristotle's system. Very roughly: there are "formal fallacies," such as illicit conversion, and "informal fallacies," such as equivocation and other *non sequiturs* stemming from linguistic confusion. But some linguistic confusions run deep and call for investigation—"conceptual investigation." Broadly defined, logic is any conceptual investigation.

Logic as conceptual investigation coincides with philosophy as inquiry into fundamental concepts. Parmenides, Zeno, and Socrates initiated logic in that sense; Plato and Aristotle developed it into a high art. In recent times Wittgenstein and others have refined this art and stressed its "grammatical" nature.

Philosophy and Grammar

Does Wittgenstein go too far? Does he reduce "love of wisdom" to a kind of philology, a mere love of words? No. For in asking about the use of the words *mind*, *time*, etc., Wittgenstein is *thereby* asking about the nature of mind, time, etc. If (to use another example) the question is about the nature of the imagination, then we ought to ask not what happens when we imagine, but how the word "imagination" is used.[7] The question "What happens when we imagine?" misleads us into wanting the description of a process, whereas what we need in philosophy is a grammatical investigation—something to help us recall the circumstances in which we speak of "imagining something." For here, "*essence* is expressed by grammar" (*PI*, sec. 371).

In the natural sciences, the nature of one's subject is often not expressed by grammar. For example, when a science teacher asks about the nature of gold, she wants to be told not about how the word *gold* is used, but rather about the hidden atomic structure of the stuff called "gold." In philosophy, however, the subject in question will never be a kind of stuff. Never hidden, the essences investigated by philosophy will always be expressed by something already in plain view, namely the "grammar" (as Wittgenstein calls it) of the language we speak.

---

7. Based on *PI*, sec. 370.

It will be helpful to look a bit further into Wittgenstein's philosophical investigation of time:

> Augustine says in the *Confessions* "What, then, is time? If no one asks me, I know; if I want to explain it to someone who has asked, I do not know."—This could not be said about a question of natural science ("What is the specific gravity of hydrogen?" for instance). Something that we know when no one asks us, but no longer know when we are supposed to give an account of it, is something that we need to *remind* ourselves of. (And it is obviously something of which for some reason it is difficult to remind oneself.) (*PI*, sec. 89, translating Augustine's Latin)

Bewitched by the fact that the word *time* is a substantive, we want to be able to designate a corresponding "substance"; unable to do so, we conclude that there is something very mysterious about time. We feel as if we had to penetrate a mysterious phenomenon, and for this reason it seems irrelevant to remind ourselves of something so mundane as the grammar of everyday language. But in fact it is relevant, for it is precisely the lack of a clear view of grammar that generates the deceptive feeling of being in the presence of something mysterious and ethereal.

Wittgenstein would say that disclosing the essence of time calls not for a theory, nor for a definition, but for a "grammatical overview." In the following extended passage, Friedrich Waismann, a one-time collaborator of Wittgenstein's, provides such an overview by recollecting the sorts of things one learned in nursery school:

> Imagine a child with a book showing a series of pictures representing the rising, culminating, and setting of the sun. Suppose he learns the words "morning," "midday," "afternoon," etc. in connection with these and related pictures.
>
> Now he learns the game of lifting his hand on the command "Lift your hand when I say 'Now'."
>
> We draw his attention to the changes in a traffic light and prompt him to guess which color will come next. He learns the tenses of a verb in connection with this game. ("The green light was showing," "The amber is showing," "The red will show next.")
>
> Now he learns to tell the time from a clock, and becomes familiar with such expressions as "In five minutes," "At twelve sharp," etc.
>
> Once these preliminary ideas are explained, we can introduce the general word "time."

So Waismann responds to the "What is time?" question not by giving a definition but with a story about how certain "preliminary ideas" might be learned and used. Then he connects these ideas with the word *time* and puts it into various contexts of use. He thereby reminds us of the word's meaning. Augustine's question was misleading because it made us expect the wrong kind of answer.[8]

Many philosophical problems are questions of the form "What is *x*?" for whose resolution we need to recollect the grammar of "*x*," that is, its use in the language. Prominent "values of *x*" from the history of philosophy include: "being," "change," "number," "color," "time," "mind," "pain," "piety," "soul," "knowledge," "opposition," etc. As there are various kinds of words, so there are various expressions of the grammar of words. These include: tables and diagrams (truth tables, etc.), samples (e.g., color samples), sets of examples (e.g., of various types of number), stories about how the use of a word was taught and learned (as in the Waismann passage), and definitions (e.g., "Opposites can't both be true").

Philosophical investigation recollects the grammar of terms that are deeply embedded in everyday language; it also conducts "a battle against the bewitchment of our intelligence by means of language." Language bewitches the intelligence by way of its outward form or "surface grammar." For example, the fact that "time" is a noun formation leads us to misconstrue its "depth grammar"—that is, to misunderstand the kind of use it actually has in what we say and do.[9]

Object and Designation

The outward forms of many words call to mind a certain primitive schema: "the model of object and designation."[10] We saw how this schema generates conceptual perplexities when applied to the terms "becoming," "motion," "time," and "pain"—perplexities expressed in the form of questions:

1) An apple ripens. How is it possible? How can what is *not red* become *red*?

2) Where is the moving arrow? At any given time it is somewhere—and so at rest.

3) One cannot measure what is not fully present. So how do we measure the past-present-future of *time*?

4) Is what I call "pain" when I hit my thumb with a hammer like what *you* call "pain" when you do the same thing? How could we possibly know?

8. I have pruned and paraphrased the much longer passage in Waismann's *The Principles of Linguistic Philosophy*, pp. 172–174.
9. See *PI*, sec. 664, for the "surface/depth grammar" distinction, and *PI*, sec. 109, for the passage from which the "bewitchment" quote was taken.
10. A phrase from *PI*, sec. 293.

These puzzles have played an important and distinctive part in the Western philosophical tradition. Parmenides and Zeno ("the Eleatics") are associated with the first and second puzzles; Augustine and modern philosophers with the third and fourth, respectively. The Eleatic puzzles arose from reflection on natural philosophy from Thales to Heraclitus; the Augustinian, from reflection on the biblical world view; the modern, from reflection on the mathematical universe of Galilean-Cartesian physics and on the subject claiming to know it. As Aristotle demonstrated a nonreductive way of resolving paradoxes in ancient thought, so Wittgenstein demonstrates a nonreductive way of resolving analogous paradoxes in medieval and modern thought.

CHAPTER TWO

The Philosophical Investigations

I am not trying to persuade you to change your opinion. I am only trying to recommend a certain sort of investigation.

—*Lectures on the Foundations of Mathematics*, p. 103

PHILOSOPHICAL INVESTIGATION

Philosophy is a process of investigation. Philosophical investigation is like trying to regain one's bearings in a familiar landscape that has come to seem strange. Writing philosophy is like presenting sketches of a landscape made in the course of long and involved journeys.

This is the picture suggested in the preface to Wittgenstein's second major work, the *Philosophical Investigations*.[1] He had said of philosophy in the *Tractatus*, his first book, that it is "not a body of doctrine but an activity," not a set of "philosophical propositions" but a process of clarifying propositions.[2] This conception is carried over into his post-*Tractatus* writings, where, from 1929 until his death in 1951, he modifies, purifies, and supplements his earlier methods of elucidation.

Wittgenstein took the motto for his *Philosophical Investigations* from the following lines in a nineteenth-century Austrian play:

There are so many means of extirpating and eradicating, and nevertheless so little evil has been extirpated . . . that one clearly sees

---

1. Although "January, 1945" is the date Wittgenstein wrote at the end of his preface, parts of the published text ("Part II," in particular) were added later. See the "Editors' Note," and Schulte, *Wittgenstein*, ch. 1. The *Investigations* were published only in 1953, two years after the author's death. Of all his major philosophical writings, only the *Tractatus* (1921) was published in Wittgenstein's lifetime.

2. See *TLP*, 4.112.

9

that people invent a lot of things, but not the right one. And yet
we live in an era of progress, don't we? I s'pose progress is like a
newly discovered land; a flourishing colonial system on the coast,
the interior still wilderness, steppe, and prairie. *It is in the nature of
all progress that it looks much greater than it really is.*[3]

Compare with the following lines from Wittgenstein's forward to his major
"transitional work," the *Philosophical Remarks* (1930):

This book is written for such men as are in sympathy with its spirit.
This spirit is different from the one which informs the vast stream
of European and American civilization in which all of us stand.
That spirit expresses itself in an onwards movement, in building
ever larger and more complicated structures; the other in striving
after clarity and perspicuity in no matter what structure. (p. 7)

The spirit animating his own work, he added, "remains where it is and what it
tries to grasp is always the same." And to judge from that, Wittgenstein had
not yet adopted the more "peripatetic" ("criss-crossing-the-landscape") conception of philosophical activity that characterizes *PI*. The more "sedentary"
conception expressed in the *Remarks* seems connected with an idea characteristic of the earlier works (and firmly rejected later, from 1932 onward): the
idea that by contemplating a particular luminous case, one might perceive the
essence of language itself. I think here of what he said in a 1913 notebook
about feeling that he had seen the essence of the proposition in the accident
models used in Paris law courts (*NB*, p. 7), and of the following passage from
the 1940s:

The basic evil of Russell's logic, as also of mine in the *Tractatus*, is
that what a proposition is is illustrated by a few commonplace
examples, and then presupposed as understood in full generality.
(*RPP*-I, sec. 38)

This "basic evil" is certainly one of the "grave errors" alluded to in the preface
to the *Investigations*. And the "wide ranging travels" that follow are meant to
remedy it.

Allied to this basic evil is a certain "craving for generality" that
expresses itself in a reluctance to look into the variety and detail of our linguistic practices.[4] Wittgenstein thought it important to overcome this craving

---

3. From Johann Nestroy's *Der Schützling* (*The Protégé*), act 4, scene 10. The last line is
the motto. (My emphasis.) I have profited throughout from the very detailed commen-
taries by Baker and Hacker. Information on the motto and the translation of Nestroy is
from their first volume, *Wittgenstein: Understanding and Meaning*.
4. See BB, pp. 17-18.

for (I think) two reasons: first because it works against the clarity we need in order to get reoriented in our thought-world or "city of language" (*PI*, sec. 18); second, because it works against a kind of ethico-religious spirit that Wittgenstein very much admired—a spirit that is well expressed, I think, in verses from Longfellow that Wittgenstein once considered taking as the motto for *PI*:

> In the elder days of art,
> Builders wrought with greatest care
> Each minute and unseen part,
> For the gods are everywhere.[5]

Wittgenstein had enormous respect for those old builders for whom "God is in the details." And he certainly emulates them in his later writings.

It seems to me that there is another, even more important religiousness in all of his works, early and late—an attitude that expresses itself in an intense striving for purity of heart. Wittgenstein wanted to dedicate all his work (indeed his life) to something beyond either "having a good time" or self-aggrandizement. He expresses this ideal with simple eloquence in the second, final, paragraph of his foreword to the *Remarks*. He would like to be able, he tells us, to dedicate his book "to the glory of God." But as now we live in dark times (far removed from "the elder days of art"), such a dedication "would not be rightly understood." Rightly understood, it would mean "that the book is written in good will." Insofar as it is not so written, but (for example) out of vanity, then "the author would wish to see it condemned."

Wittgenstein's religion is to be found less in what he says, more in the spirit in which he says it. As his philosophy is not in philosophical theses, so his religion is not in religious doctrines. But while his philosophy is to be found in a certain (elucidatory) activity, his religion is a spirit that pervades (or is meant to pervade) that and other activities of his life: a spirit that seeks clarity as an end in itself, not as a means—not for the sake of "adding one construction to another, moving on and up" (PR, p. 7).[6]

---

5. From "The Builders." Quoted in *CV*, p. 34 (dated 1938).

6. "The real discovery is the one that . . . gives philosophy peace" (*PI*, sec. 133). Yes, but this "peace" is *internally* related to "the spirit that seeks *clarity* as an end." (Cf. CV, p. 7: "I am not interested in constructing a building, so much as in having a perspicuous view of the foundations of possible buildings. / So I am not aiming at the same target as the scientists and my way of thinking is different from theirs." The "buildings" of modern thinkers may have reminded Wittgenstein of the biblical Tower of Babel.)

As the goal of philosophy is not "philosophical propositions" but making propositions clear, so the goal of religion is not "religious activities" but doing whatever one does without vanity, "to the glory of God." Wittgenstein compares language to an old city with many districts (*PI*, sec. 18). If religion has any district of its own in "the city of language," it is not described in the *Investigations*. Here, as in the *Tractatus*, religion is essentially "mystical," wordless.

"Obviously the essence of religion cannot have anything to do with the fact that there is talking," said Wittgenstein in a 1930 conversation with Friedrich Waismann. "Or rather," he added, "when people talk, then this itself is part of a religious act and not a theory. Thus it also does not matter at all if the words used are true or false or nonsense" (*WVC*, p. 117). So, insofar as distinctively religious words really enter into the life of the city, they will function either "ceremonially" (in set ceremonies of worship, confession, prayer, and thanksgiving) or "grammatically," in the course of teaching people a new way of living and assessing life.[7]

As the major difficulty for most readers of the *Investigations* is that of not see- ing the woods for the trees, my goal has been to clearly bring out some of the main lines of Wittgenstein's thought. So I have not tried to produce a com- plete commentary, nor to say something about each and every section.

Several sets of lecture notes from Wittgenstein's students are now avail- able in print, together with collections of remarks from his *Nachlaß*. I draw on this material extensively for help in interpreting and fleshing out the *Investigations*.

Although much of what I say is in commentary style, I sometimes use dialogue form, so as to bring out the essentially "dialogical" character of Wittgenstein's thought.

Part I of the *Investigations* consists of short sections on language (secs. 1–242) and mind (secs. 243–693); Part II, of fourteen longer sections (i–xiv) on psychological concepts and philosophy of psychology. The commentary to follow is also divided into two major parts: "Language" and "Mind," with the latter drawing from both parts of Wittgenstein's work.

LANGUAGE

Pictures of the Essence of Language
*(Sections 1–64)**

WORDS AS POINTING FINGERS (SECTIONS 1–5)
"When Augustine talks about the learning of language he talks about how we attach names to things, or understand the names of things. *Naming* here

---

* Section numbers refer to sections of *Investigations*, Part I.
7. I develop these themes in the final two chapters.

appears as the foundation, the be all and end all of language" (*PG*, p. 56). This "philosophical picture" of the way language functions goes along with the "philosophical concept of meaning" according to which every word has a meaning, in the sense of something correlated with it for which it stands.[8]

The *picture* is called "philosophical" because it generates the philosophical concept; the *concept* is called "philosophical" because it generates paradigm cases of philosophical problems, such as Augustine's famous: "What is time? If you don't ask me, I know; if you ask me, I don't know."[9] (If we know what a fortnight is, we can *say*. If we want to explain what "chair" means, we can point to something. "Time" is more mysterious because nothing seems to *correspond* to it that we can say or point to.)

One could say: Augustine had a "primitive idea of the way language functions." Or one could speak more charitably and say: Augustine had "the idea of a language more primitive than ours." The important thing is that his idea is appropriate *only* for a narrowly circumscribed region of language. In order to define this area, Wittgenstein imagines a language more primitive than our own, "the builder's language" (sec. 2). *There* it certainly does make sense to see words as substitutes for the pointing gesture.

The shopping language of sec. 1 involves three kinds of words. It is offered as a reminder to Augustine of something he tends to overlook: the variety of ways in which we operate with words. (And Augustine represents the philosopher in all of us.) The philosophical concept of the meaning of a word surrounds the workings of language in a fog. It disperses the fog to look at simple, "primitive" cases, such as the shopping language, where we command a clear view of the ways words function.[10]

Instruction in primitive forms of language consists in *training*. This training forms a "bedrock" (sec. 217) on which more sophisticated forms of language can be built up. (That the shopper of sec. 1 had learned a series of numbers by rote [*auswendig*] is part of what enabled him to go to the store to buy five red apples. It is also part of what he will need to learn arithmetic.)

How was the shopper able to fill the order to obtain five *red* apples?

---

8. In the early '30s Wittgenstein confessed to having himself been under the spell of the view he here attributes to Augustine: "The concept of meaning I adopted . . . originates in a primitive philosophy of language" (*PG*, p. 56). He added that in German "meaning" is derived from "pointing." So we might call the primitive philosophy he shared with Augustine "the pointing finger picture." (Why does *PI* open with Augustine? Wittgenstein lived through the decline and fall of an empire and civilization; I wonder if the thought that Augustine experienced something similar made him seem a kindred spirit. Compare Malcolm's *Memoir*, p. 71.)

9. *Confessions* XI, 14.

10. Wittgenstein acknowledges a great debt to the criticism of the Cambridge econo-

[H]e looks up the word "red" in a table and finds a color sample opposite it. . . . "But how does he know where and how he is to look up the word 'red' . . . ?"—Well, I assume that he *acts* as I have described. Explanations come to an end somewhere. (sec. 1)

Here explanations come to an end when we remind the questioner of the kind of training the shopper received.

Wittgenstein here uses the term *explanation* in the sense in which explanation and justification are two sides of the same coin. If we ask the shopper to justify his claim to have fetched apples of the right color, he may use the color chart. If we press him to justify his use of that, he may now have the right to say: "I have exhausted the justifications, have reached bedrock, and my spade is turned. This is simply what I do."[11]

OSTENSIVE TEACHING (SECTIONS 6–7)

The idea that "individual words in language name objects" is associated with a particular view of how language would have to be learned, namely by way of "ostension," pointing. Pointing gestures are in fact involved in language instruction. This "ostensive" behavior is of two kinds: "ostensive teaching," used to introduce toddlers to many primitive forms of language, and "ostensive definition," employed only at a later stage. The former is a kind of *training*; the latter, a kind of *explanation*. All early language instruction is training, for giving and understanding explanations presupposes a language already. Thus: "in a certain sense, the use of language is something that cannot be taught, i.e. I cannot use language to teach it in the way in which language could be used to teach someone to play the piano" (*PR*, p. 54).

Distinguish *instruction in language*, such as ostensive teaching, from *the practice of the use of language*, as when the builder gives orders and the assistant

---

mist Piero Sraffa (*PI*, p. vi). I imagine the focus of the criticism was the "primitive philosophy of language" he then shared with Augustine. Perhaps it was this criticism that prompted him "to study the phenomena of language in primitive kinds of application." For Sraffa would have used that sort of study in his own investigations, to disperse the fog surrounding the workings of the economy. ("Let us consider an extremely simple society which produces just enough to maintain itself. . . . / Suppose at first that only two commodities are produced, wheat and iron. Both are used, in part as sustenance for those who work, and the rest as means of production. . . . / [E]xchange values . . . spring directly from the methods of production." Thus begins Sraffa's *Production of Commodities by Means of Commodities*, p. 3.)

11. *PI*, sec. 217, paraphrased. Cf. sec. 289: "To use a word without a justification does not mean to use it without right." Compare the very important sec. 5 with the following texts: "To what extent can the function of language be described? If someone is not master of a language, I may bring him to a mastery of it by training. Someone who is master of it, I may remind of the kind of training . . . " (*RFM*, p. 333). "Language did not emerge from some kind of ratiocination" (*OC*, sec. 475).

obeys them. Think of naming—and of the ostention connected with it—not as the essence of human language but as a preparation for it.

ADDITIONS TO THE HOUSE OF LANGUAGE (SECTIONS 8–9)

In these sections numerals ("a," "b," etc.), demonstratives (e.g., "this"), and color samples are added to the "builder's language" of sec. 2. Syntax also appears. This can be seen in the fact that some combinations, e.g., "b-slab-there" would say something while others, e.g., "slab-there-b," would not. (Proper names will be added in section 15.)

WORDS AS TOOLS (SECTIONS 10–17)

Consider the words of our own language. That they all look very much alike disguises the fact that they are really as different as the various tools in a tool-box. Just as nothing would be gained by saying that all tools have the same function, "to *modify* something," so (by analogy) nothing would be gained by saying that all words have the same function, "to *signify* something."

In the expanded primitive language of sec. 8, the builder shows his assistant color samples in the course of giving him orders. These and other samples may be counted among the "tools of language."[12]

Is all this leading up to a pragmatic, instrumentalist theory of language? No. The point of the comparison of words with tools is simply to highlight features of language that were obscured by the comparison of words with pointing fingers.

LIFE IN THE CITY OF LANGUAGE (SECTIONS 18–24)

Language is inseparable from activities such as commanding, greeting, recounting, asking, etc. As we learn to participate in these activities, we learn our native language; as we learn our native language, we learn not only *forms of words* but also *forms of life*. We learn to *act* in such-and-such ways—to (for example) punish certain actions, establish a fact, give orders, render accounts, tell the time, take an interest in people's feelings, etc.

A form of life is to a form of words what a tool's function is to a tool's appearance. ("If I had to say what is the main mistake made by philosophers of the present generation . . . I would say that it is that when language is looked

---

12. A scarlet spot might function as a sample of what we call "scarlet." Similarly—as is remarked at the foot of *PI*, p. 7—the words "This is an English sentence" might function as a sample of what we call "an English sentence." Now compare that self-referential use of language with Russell's infamous: "This sentence is false." Do *those* words have a self-referential use? If you say yes, you need to explain what it is. For it is hard to see how they could function on the model of "This is an English sentence," as a *sample* of something. (Cf. Z, sec. 691 and Mounce's *Introduction*, pp. 121–123.)

at, what is looked at is a form of words, and not the use made of the form of words" [*LC*, p. 2].)

In the language game of sec. 2, a builder calls out "slab" and his assistant brings him a slab. Is he speaking *elliptically*? We will say no if we focus on forms of life—on what the builders *do* with "slab." We will say yes if we focus on forms of words—on how "slab" looks; for, in our language, we expect a sentence to be complex—"a combination of names" (sec. 1).

From the shopping illustration in the final paragraph of sec. 1 onwards, we have been given examples of words at work. In section 7 "the whole, consisting of language and the actions into which they are woven" was called "the language game." Here the term "language *game*" ("Sprach*spiel*") is meant to emphasize that the *speaking* of language ("the practice of the use of language") is "part of an activity, or of a form of life" (sec. 23 b).[13]

Although there is no fixed, closed list of language games, there are examples: "Giving orders and obeying them. . . . Asking, thanking, greeting, cursing, praying." These and similar proceedings are to be called "language games" (cf. sec. 69).

Language games are many and various. Philosophers seeking to elucidate the logic of our language need to notice this variety and multiplicity. There are just many more language games than are dreamt of in their philosophies.

For the old "picture of the essence of human language," according to which words name objects and sentences picture facts, we are to substitute this new one: language is an enormous fabric of activities that involve the use of words, sentences, and other symbols. And for the old picture according to which the essence of learning a language is a matter of learning names for objects, we are to substitute this new one: learning a language is being initiated into human life—i.e., into the practices of naming, calling, indicating a choice, counting things, measuring the length of a stick, telling time, etc., etc.[14]

TALKING AND THINKING (SECTION 25)

In sec. 2. we were asked to conceive the giving-and-obeying-orders of the builder and his assistant as "a complete primitive language." It might be

---

13. It would be misleading to speak, as some do, of "Wittgenstein's language-game theory." His various uses of the term do not add up to a theory. (Compare its use in sec. 7 with its use here and in the next paragraph.) At the end of a 1939 course in philosophy of mathematics, Wittgenstein voiced the fear that his teaching might succeed only in "sowing the seeds of a new jargon." I fear this has been the fate of "language game" and "forms of life"—terms now commonly employed in facile justifications of relativism.

14. The last few lines draw heavily from Cavell's *The Claim of Reason*, pp. 177–178.

objected that Wittgenstein left out the crucial fact that these people must also *think*. For unless they were like us in that respect, they would be behaving in a purely mechanical way, like robots. To this objection, Wittgenstein later responded that it is of course true

> that the life of those men must be like ours in many respects, and that [in *PI*, sec. 2] I said nothing about this similarity. But the important thing is that their language, and their thinking too, may be rudimentary, that there is such a thing as "primitive thinking" which is to be described via primitive *behavior*.[15]

What makes the sounds they utter linguistic rather than merely mechanical is—not the inner "thinking accompaniment" of their speech—but the wider circumstances of their life.

"But surely language is founded on thought!" Why say that when we normally deduce the ability to think from the ability to talk, not vice versa? "But don't we explain the lower animals' incapacity for language by their inability to think?" The lower animals simply don't use language, except in its most rudimentary forms; commanding, questioning, recounting, chatting, and the like are no part of their natural history.

(Shall we say: "The builder's assistant doesn't think; he just does what he was *trained* to do"? No. If he can obey the builder's orders, he can also disobey them; so he may not always do what he was trained to do. And even if he does, that does not make him mindless—any more than children always counting as they are trained to do makes *them* mindless.)

NAMING (SECTIONS 26–37)

Naming is not the essence of language learning but a preparation for it. What, precisely, the naming is preparation *for* will vary with the kind of name involved. (Recall that each name in the "five red apples" language game of sec. 1 was taught and used differently.)

If a noun names a person, place, or thing, then what does the noun "time" name? Though we can *find* nothing, the word's noun form tempts us to think there must *be* something:

> Talk about a chair and a human body and all is well; talk about negation and the human mind and things begin to look queer. A substantive in language is used primarily for a physical body, and a verb for the movement of such a body. This is the simplest application of language, and this fact is immensely important. When we have difficulty with the grammar of our language we take certain

---

15. From *Z*, sec. 99. Compare "the builders" of *PI*, sec. 2 with "the feeble-minded" of *Z*, sec. 372.

primitive schemas and try to give them wider application than is possible. (*WLA*, p. 119)

"THIS" (SECTIONS 38–42)

According to logical atomism, the view of language Wittgenstein once shared with his teacher Bertrand Russell, "you can get down in theory, if not practice, to ultimate simples, out of which the world is built, and these simples have a kind of reality not belonging to anything else."[16] Wittgenstein's critique of this philosophical concept of meaning extends from these sections through sec. 64.

The legendary King Arthur had a sword named "Excalibur" (sec. 44). We can make meaningful statements about Excalibur even though it does not now and perhaps never did exist. Now, according to logical atomism, it is possible to make meaningful statements about nonexistent or destructible objects only because they are analyzable into statements about what cannot be destroyed and must exist—i.e., about those "ultimate simples" said to have "a kind of reality not belonging to anything else." Russell called any word that actually named one of these very special, indestructible objects a "logically proper name." Although the names used in everyday, ordinary language are not "logically proper names," they must—to the extent they are meaningful— be analyzable into them.

From the perspective of logical atomism, a language that never "gets down to simples" will always look incomplete (sec. 2); everything we ordinarily say will appear elliptical (secs. 19–20). For when do we use "logically proper names"? If the answer is *never*, how can we spell out fully what we want to say?

Russell once said that the demonstrative pronoun "this" might be the only true logically proper name. What could have lead him to say such an extraordinary thing? Perhaps he was under the spell of the primitive philosophy of language according to which:

> naming = pointing ("demonstration," "ostension")
> a word's meaning = what it names ("its bearer").

For if these philosophical equations are applied to the grammatical fact that the demonstrative pronouns must always be used in the presence of a bearer, the implication is that the only *real* names may be pronouns.

It is as though Russell were determined to confuse the function of one kind of word with that of another. For isn't a name—in contrast with a

---

16. From Russell's *The Philosophy of Logical Atomism*, beginning of the final lecture.

demonstrative pronoun—precisely the kind of word that can function in the *absence* of a bearer?

> The demonstrative "this" can never be used without a bearer. . . .
> But that does not make the word into a name. . . . [F]or a name is
> not used with, but only explained by means of, the gesture of
> pointing. (sec. 45)

Consider the names of colors: we do not normally point to samples when we are actually using them to describe the appearance of objects, etc.; we do normally point to samples when we are *instructing* someone in their use. We do not have to be pointing at anything when we say that absinthe is chartreuse, as we do when we say "*This* is chartreuse."

While a few words are used only in the presence of bearers, most are not. And while sometimes the meaning of a word is defined by pointing to something or someone "corresponding to it" (sec. 43 b), often it is not. In no case is a word's meaning to be *equated* with its bearer. ("When Mr. N. N. dies one says that the bearer of the name dies, not that the meaning dies" [sec. 40].)

THE MEANING OF A WORD (SECTION 43)

"[T]he meaning of a word is its use in the language" (sec. 43 a). In order to test this definition, what are we to look at—if not at the use of "meaning" in the language? And we will find a variety of cases if we look at the use.[17]

Contrast "the meaning of a word in the language" with "what *you* mean by a word." Although "bububu" has no use in the language, you may give it a use in your private code.[18]

Contrast asking for the meaning of a word with asking for the meaning of a change in blood pressure. "The meaning of *x*" is "the use of *x* in the language" only if *x* is a word or other "instrument of the language."

(Does the phrase "the meaning of a word" always refer to the use of the word? No. There is "a secondary sense" of the phrase in which it is used to express an immediate experience or reaction. Imagine being so impressed by the blueness of a sky that you exclaim: "Now I know what 'blue' *really* means!" But it is only someone who, in one sense, already knows the meaning of "blue" who could express himself in that way. So the sense in which the meaning of a word is *not* its use in the language presupposes a sense in which it *is*.[19])

SENTENCES AS COMBINATIONS OF NAMES (SECTIONS 46–52)

"The essence of speech is the composition of names": this pronouncement from Plato's *Theaetetus* is reminiscent of logical atomism, which says that, in

---

17. See Hanfling, *Wittgenstein's Later Philosophy*, pp. 42–48.
18. See the passages printed beneath the line on *PI*, p. 18.
19. On the "primary/secondary sense" distinction, see *PI*, p. 216 and sec. 282.

the final analysis, names must refer to "the *absolutely simple* elements or objects out of which reality is composed." But what are these "simple constituent parts of reality"?—It may help to begin with the more down-to-earth question: What are the simple constituent parts of a chair?

> "Simple" [Wittgenstein observes] means: not composite. And here the point is: in what sense "composite"? It makes no sense at all to speak absolutely of the "simple parts of a chair." (sec. 47)

"This is composite" says nothing unless what is to be counted "simple" and what "composite" has already been determined. The point of the simple/composite contrast is given only *within* a language game.[20]

Section 48 presents a language game for which the *Theaetetus* pronouncement is really valid. *Here* a sentence truly is a complex of names corresponding to a complex of elements:

> The primary elements are the colored squares. "But are these simple?"—I do not know what else you would have me call "the simples." . . . But under other circumstances I should call the monochrome square "composite," consisting perhaps of two rectangles, or of the elements color and shape.

When words are taken out of the context in which they do their normal work, then "language is like an engine idling" (sec. 132). But then we need to supply a context for them, by inventing a language game for them to operate in. Wittgenstein does this for the words "simple" and "complex" in this section. He "brings words back from their metaphysical use" (sec. 116). For words in their "metaphysical use" have the mere semblance of sense.

"The elements are ineffable, and can only be named." How about transforming this metaphysical pronouncement into something less mystifying? For example: "when in a limiting case a complex consists of only *one* square, its description is simply the name of the colored square" (sec. 49).

"Neither being nor non-being is attributable to the elements." What could this mean? "One might say," Wittgenstein suggests, "that if everything that we call 'being' and 'non-being' consists in the existence and non-existence of connections between elements, [then] it makes no sense to speak of *elements* being ([or] non-being)" (sec. 50). One is tempted, he continues, to add a metaphysical explanation to this: namely, "that existence cannot be attributed to an element, for if it did not *exist*, one could not even name it and so could say nothing at all of it." Thus arises the metaphysical notion that there must be objects that not merely exist (contingently), but necessarily

---

20. Compare BB, pp. 45–46.

exist (timelessly). To de-mystify this notion, Wittgenstein presents an analogy:

> There is *one* thing of which one can say neither that it is one meter long, nor that it is not one meter long, and that is the standard meter in Paris. (sec. 50)

"The standard meter bar has the extraordinary property of being both a meter and *not* a meter long!" If this is nonsensical (as clearly it is), then (by analogy) it is equally nonsensical to say that the "elements" of the sec. 48 language game are "beyond being and non-being."

Suppose we played a language game that employed standard color samples as instruments of color predication, as now (suppose) we use "the standard meter" as an instrument of measuring. If we were asked to explain the meaning of "sepia," we would point to the appropriate hermetically sealed sample and say: "It's the name of *that* color." What, now, if someone were to say: "If that sample did not exist, it could have no name"? Would that be to say any more than that if it did not exist, we could not use it in our language game?

> What looks as if it *had* to exist is part of the language. It is a paradigm in our language game; something with which comparison is made. And this may be an important observation; but it is nonetheless an observation concerning our language game—our method of representation. (sec. 50)

(Compare *Zettel*, secs. 458-459:

> Philosophical investigations: conceptual investigations. The essential thing about metaphysics: it obliterates the distinction between factual and conceptual investigations. The fundamental thing [for a conceptual investigation is] expressed grammatically . . . ")

In sec. 48, the signs "R," "B," etc. were said to correspond to colored squares. "But what does the correspondence between signs and what they signify consist in?" Here we need to describe the language game in which the signs function, not to make conjectures about it. In other words: we need a grammatical investigation, not a metaphysical theory.

RULES (SECTIONS 53–54)

The *Theaetetus* language game was constructed according to rules expressed in a table. Such a table might be referred to in the actual use of language (to justify the application of a term), as well as in instruction for its use.

As rules are involved in various ways in games, so rules are involved in various ways in language. Sometimes the players and speakers refer to tables, definitions, or other expressions of rules, sometimes not. If, in the latter case, we still say that they play the game or speak the language according to definite rules, that will be because we have "read off" such-and-such rules by observing them play or speak.[21]

METAPHYSICS (SECTIONS 55–59)

In one sense of this confusing word, "metaphysics" is the effort to describe "the *a priori*—universal, necessary, trans-empirical—structure of reality." What it turns out to be describing, however, is only (as it were) a reflection of linguistic facts.

"While red things can be destroyed, redness itself cannot be destroyed; that is why the meaning of the word 'red' is independent of the existence of a red thing." Wittgenstein responds to this bit of platonist metaphysics by uncovering the sort of linguistic fact it reflects:

> Certainly it makes no sense to say that the color red is torn up or pounded to bits. . . . [But] suppose you cannot remember the color any more? —When we forget which color this is the name of, ... we are no longer able to play a particular language game with it. And the situation then is comparable with that in which we have lost a paradigm [standard sample] which was an instrument of our language. (sec. 57)

Our platonist begins with wonder at the fact that it makes no sense to say that redness is destroyed—a wonder he proceeds to express in the form of the question, "How is this possible?" If he accepts the preceding "translation" of that philosophical question, he will no longer feel compelled to go beyond the linguistic ("grammatical") facts it describes. For then the fact from which he began will no longer strike him as *peculiarly* marvelous. And so he will no longer see his "theory of forms"—or indeed any theory—as an answer to his earlier "How is this possible?" question. For then he will see it as a symptom of a deep grammatical confusion.

(Wittgenstein's notorious "antimetaphysical stance" is really the rejection of a certain classical and contemporary approach to philosophical problems and their solutions. It should not be confused with the rejection of "otherworldly" philosophies of life.)

ANALYSIS (SECTIONS 60–64)

The conception of philosophical analysis associated with logical atomism involves thinking of the analyzed form of a proposition as more fundamental than the unanalyzed form. In the *Tractatus* this led to the idea that there are

---

21. But how does the observer of a game distinguish mistakes from correct play? and what's the difference between "laws of nature" and "rules of a game"? Upcoming sections on rules speak to these and related questions: secs. 80–86, 108, 142, and 138–242. Cf. *BB*, pp. 12–13, and Schulte's *Wittgenstein*, p. 115.

"elementary propositions" hidden in language, which it is the job of philosophical analysis to dig out. Here Wittgenstein objects that some aspects of things are lost through analysis. He gives the example of the French flag: a foreigner may see it as simply as an arrangement of blue, white, and red rectangles; a French patriot, as something with "a quite special character" (sec. 64).

In these sections Wittgenstein is disavowing a view that had shaped his thinking in the *Tractatus*: the view that there must be a fundamental description of the world to which all other meaningful description is to be reduced. I take it that this view, "logical atomism," is one of the "grave mistakes" referred to in the preface to the *Investigations* (p. vi).[22]

Logic and Philosophy
(Sections 65–137)

"[The reason] the problems of philosophy . . . are posed is that the logic of our language is misunderstood" (*TLP*, p. 3).

GAMES AND FAMILIES (SECTIONS 65–71)

The early Wittgenstein tended to take an "essentialist" view of common nouns: the view that there *must* be some common element in all cases in which we apply such a word, something that regulates our use of it for all those cases. The later Wittgenstein challenges this requirement by describing counterexamples, starting with "game":

> Consider . . . board games, card games, ball games, Olympic games, and so on. . . . [I]f you look at them you will not see something that is common to *all*, but similarities, relationships, and a whole series of them at that. (sec. 66)

The same is true for *language* games: when we look at examples (as in secs. 2, 8, 15, 48), we will not find the kind of "essence" that essentialists say must be there. We will find something akin to *family resemblances*:

> We are inclined to think that there must be something in common to all games, say, and that this common property is the justification for applying the general term "game" to the various games; whereas [in fact] games form a *family* the members of which have family likenesses. Some of them have the same nose, others the same eyebrows and others again the same way of walking; and these likenesses overlap. (*BB*, p. 17)

"In the absence of a definition that specifies sharply what counts as games and what not, isn't the use of the term unregulated?" (sec. 68, paraphrased). No. The lack of such a specification doesn't mean that anything

---

22. See Cora Diamond's "Losing Your Concepts" for interesting examples of the many *different* kinds of activity we call "description."

goes. Nor does it make the concept less usable in practice. (My wife tells me to show the children a game, and I teach them gaming with dice. "That's not the sort of game I meant!," she objects. It would be no excuse to respond: "But you didn't specify that in advance!"[23])

Is a "war game" a game? "We do not know the boundaries because none have been drawn. . . . [W]e can draw a boundary—for a special purpose. [But] does it take that to make the concept usable?" (sec. 69; cf. sec. 88).

POINTING OUT A COMMON PROPERTY (SECTIONS 72–74)

You show me two paintings composed of many patches of color, telling me that the one color found in both is called "mauve." If you proceed to send me to the store for mauve fabric and then challenge what I buy, I might try to justify my purchase by holding it up against a patch of the color found in both of the paintings you showed me. This would be a case of (successfully or unsuccessfully) justifying my application of a general name by pointing out a common property.

I show you samples of different shades of blue and say "The color common to all of these is called 'blue.'" This would *not* be justifying my application of a term by pointing out a common property. "All blue things are blue" is a tautology.[24]

KNOWING AND SAYING (SECTIONS 75–78)

Does knowing what something is imply the ability to say what one knows? It depends. If we look at a variety of cases, we will not want to insist that whoever knows something must always be able to say what he knows. Compare:

- How many meters high a mountain is
- What "troglodyte" means
- How the word *game* is used (*PI*, sec. 66)
- How "beautiful" and "ugly" are used
- How coffee smells (*PI*, sec. 610)

Here as elsewhere our concepts turn out to be more complicated than we tend to expect.

Many everyday concepts have "blurred" (*PI*, sec. 77) or "ragged" (*CV*, p. 45) boundaries. Drawing a sharp boundary around such concepts would seriously distort them in many cases. (A recent book by Hans Sluga tells of how the Third Reich, aided and abetted by many of its philosophers, imposed an unnatural—and tendentious—precision on such essentially blurred sociopolitical concepts as "nation" and "race."[25])

---

23. Cf. the passage at the foot of *PI*, p. 33.
24. *BB*, pp. 130–131. Cf. *PI*, secs. 67 and 72.
25. *Heidegger's Crisis*, passim.

Consider the words *beautiful* and *ugly* and notice that we use them in a hundred different language games: the beauty of a face is different from the beauty of a chair, a flower, the binding of a book, etc. Note also how the words are learned:

> We do not as children discover the quality of beauty or ugliness in a *face* and find that these are qualities a *tree* has in common with it. The words "beautiful and "ugly" are bound up with the words they modify, and when applied to a face are not the same as when applied to flowers and trees. . . . And similarly in ethics: the meaning of the word "good" is bound up with the act it modifies. (*WLA*, p. 35; cf. *PO*, p. 104)

Used to modify "human being" or "person," adjectives such as "good" and "bad" have a different sense from when they modify "pianist" or "tennis player," for example. Thus (paraphrasing *PO*, pp. 38–39): "If you tell me I play tennis badly and I answer, 'But I don't want to play any better,' all you could say would be, 'Ah then that's all right.' But if you tell me I'm not behaving like a decent human being and I answer, 'But I don't want to behave any better,' you couldn't make the same answer; you'd say, 'Well, you *ought* to want to behave better.' Here we have a judgment of ethical or absolute value, whereas the first was a judgment of relative or instrumental value."

Criticizing his colleague A.C. Ewing's definition of *good* as "what it is right to admire," Wittgenstein imagined three solid pieces of stone:

> You pick them up, fit them together and get a ball; what you now have tells you something about the three shapes. But suppose you now start with three lumps of mud. It would tell you nothing to put them together and mould a ball from them. Ewing makes a soft ball out of three formless lumps. His definition throws no light.[26]

The use of the word *good* is surprisingly complicated. We need to survey that complexity—not paper it over with a definition.[27]

"MOSES" (SECTION 79)

Although we use many names without any fixed, unvarying analysis (definition or definite description), "that detracts as little from their usefulness as it detracts from that of a table that it stands on four legs instead of three and so sometimes wobbles" (sec. 79 c). Now this applies not only to a proper name such as "Moses" (as Wittgenstein explains in the present section) but also to a general name such as "gold." That a chemical element's atomic number once

---

26. Paraphrased from Bouwsma's *Conversations*, pp. 41–42.
27. For an illuminating survey of the complexity of words such as *good*, see Hallett's book on moral reasoning, chap. 2.

counted as an empirical discovery while now it counts as a defining criterion illustrates the "fluctuation of scientific definitions" alluded to at the close of this section. And there is a similar point to be made about some non-technical general names—for example, "love":

> The same verbal expression, "This is not love, because he does not behave as if it were" can stand for a *rule*, viz., "I do not call this love because . . . ," or my saying it can mean that I do not think it is love because people do not usually behave as he did. (If as a matter of fact a certain feeling almost always goes together with a certain behavior, we are inclined to use the feeling and behavior alternatively as criteria for love. This is all right so long as we do not get into a situation in which we have to distinguish between what we mean by love: a feeling, or behavior. These are different criteria.) (WLA, pp. 90-91)[28]

NORMAL/NORMATIVE (SECTIONS 80–90)

In normal circumstances we apply common names such as "chair" without hesitation; in abnormal circumstances we might not know what to say. If asked to define "chair," we might say that it is a certain article of furniture for sitting on. But suppose there was something that looked like a chair, only to disappear just as people lower themselves onto it. We wouldn't know whether to call it a chair or not; the rules governing the use of the word "chair" do not provide for every contingency. If all chairs were like this imaginary one, "chair" would no longer serve the function in language it presently has. That is, if the world became very different, there would be no *point* in making a distinction between what we call "chairs" and other kinds of things. ("I am inclined to distinguish between the essential and the inessential in a game too. The game, one would like to say, has not only rules but also a *point*."[29])

Like games proper, language games are normative activities. Just as some chess moves are ruled out and others permitted, so some word formations are nonsense ("illogical") and others make sense. Logic (i.e., logical investigation) views human language as a rule-governed, normative practice; it tries to read off definite rules of sense and nonsense from the practice of the language game.

What sort of norms or rules govern the meaningful employment of words? "In philosophy we often *compare* the use of words with games and cal-

---

28. (I have transposed some of the sentences in this quotation.) For an illuminating discussion of criteria, see Glock, "Wittgenstein vs. Quine on Logical Necessity," in Teghrarian and Serafini, eds., *Wittgenstein and Contemporary Philosophy*, pp. 154–186. See also *PI*, secs. 353–354.
29. Sec. 564. Cf. sec. 62.

culi which have fixed rules" (sec. 81). This is useful in that it emphasizes that our interest as philosophers is directed to language as a normative activity:

> [W]e talk about it as we do about the pieces in chess when we are stating the rules of the game, not describing their physical properties. (sec. 108 c)

But we go wrong if we think that in uttering a sentence and meaning it we *must* be playing a game with fixed rules, such as chess.

The origin of baseball used to be traced back to the rule-making activity of a certain Abner Doubleday. Nowadays it is thought that baseball and its rules evolved from generations of children and adults "playing around" on a field with ball and bat. Sometimes everyday speech is more like that playing-around stage of the game than the evolved state. Although these informal games and language games *are* rule governed, they are rule governed in a way very different from the way the "more evolved" games (with their books of rules and official umpires) are rule governed.

(When we make up and even alter the rules as we go along, can we still claim to be *following* them? Is everyday, "informal" language really the normative, rule-governed practice we said it was? Can the "mouse" of logic be found among the "dust and rags" of the everyday practice of language?[30]—Much of the rest of *PI*, Part I pertains to these questions.)

Is there a language game whose rules never let a doubt creep in about the application of a word? Is there a signpost that leaves no doubt about which way to go? Must a *complete* language game have rules for the application of rules—e.g., the schemas for reading tables mentioned in sec. 86?

Definitions and other explanations of meaning are not defective just because they might prove unhelpful in abnormal circumstances; clarity and precision do not disappear with the abstract possibility of vagueness and ambiguity. Like a signpost, a definition is in order if it achieves its aim in normal circumstances.[31]

LANGUAGE AND THE IDEAL (SECTIONS 91–106)

The "What is language?" question of traditional philosophy makes us look for the essence of language in something hidden that we might "dig out" and describe—whereas what we really need is an overview of something visible on the surface of language. The essence of language—its function and structure—becomes visible by a rearrangement of what we see and hear every day in the practice of language.

---

30. Cf. sec. 52.
31. On secs. 88–90, see chap. 1, above (especially pp. 5–7).

"Propositions are remarkable!": this might express a realistic sense of their importance in our lives—or a fanciful misunderstanding of the logic of our language.

"If *p* is a proposition, then *p* means: *such and such is so and so*." But "means" is a verb—which makes it sound as if the proposition *did* something. ("'Es regnet' means the same as 'It's raining.'") It sounds as if there must be a "a something" for both sentences to mean!)

"Thought is surrounded by a halo": this was the inflated mind-set of the *Tractatus*. "Thought can be of what's *not* the case": if this truism sounds paradoxical, it is because of that inflated mind-set.[32] We need a more realistic, less fanciful approach to thought and to logic, its essence.

Is an indefinite sense no sense at all (as the early Wittgenstein claimed)?[33] Is an enclosure with a gap in it no enclosure at all? ("A man will be *imprisoned* in a room with a door that's unlocked and opens inwards; as long as it does not occur to him to *pull* rather than push it" [CV, p. 42].)

We are dazzled by The Ideal—the ideal, for instance, of a logically perfect language (where speaking a language is operating a calculus according to rigid rules). We fear that toppling the ideal would be like plucking out the very "eye of the mind"—whereas really it would be like removing a pair of glasses.

"Propositions are like pictures; facts, like configurations of objects; names, like pointing fingers."[34] Insightful as they are, the importance of these comparisons is easily exaggerated. To the early Wittgenstein, they appeared to disclose the very essence of language and the world. Readers of the later Wittgenstein must beware of supposing that he ascribes any such exaggerated importance to the comparison of words to tools and language to games.

"We predicate of the thing what lies in the method of representing it" (sec. 104). For example, in his story of Achilles and the tortoise, Zeno predicated of a race what belongs to the grammar of the series he used to represent it. From the purely grammatical point that the series of fractions never comes to an end, he fallaciously inferred that the race itself never comes to an end.[35]

We are dazzled by the ideal and therefore fail to see the actual use of words clearly. "Here it is difficult . . . to see that we must stick to the subjects of

---

32. For more on this, see my concluding chapter.
33. *TLP*, 3.23; cf. *NB*, pp. 67–68.
34. Recall that in German the word for "meaning" came from the word for "pointing" (*PG*, sec. I-19).
35. On this and related logico-philosophical paradoxes, see Waismann, *Principles of Linguistic Philosophy*, pp. 87–88, and Brenner, *Logic and Philosophy*, pp. 136–137.

our every-day thinking, and not go astray and imagine that we have to describe extreme subtleties" (sec. 106).

"BACK TO THE ROUGH GROUND!" (SECTIONS 107–108)

> A thought is a proposition with a sense. The totality of propositions is language. Man possesses the ability to construct languages capable of expressing every sense/ . . . [$\bar{p},\bar{\xi},N(\bar{\xi})$] is the general form of a proposition. What this says is just that every proposition is a result of successive applications to elementary propositions of the operation $N(\bar{\xi})$.[36]

That was from the *Tractatus*. When, in these sections of the *Investigations*, Wittgenstein acknowledges that thought lacks the formal unity he had once imagined, his "old self" breaks in with the worry: "But what becomes of logic now? Its essential purity seems to be compromised." To which the "new self" replies:

> The *preconceived idea* of crystalline purity can only be removed by turning our whole examination round. (One might say: the axis of reference of our examination must be rotated, but about the fixed point of our real need.) (sec. 108)

The *Tractatus* viewed all significant use of words as timelessly fixed by "the general form of the proposition." And behind that view was this picture:

> Thought is surrounded by a halo.—Its essence, logic, presents the order of *possibilities*, which must be *utterly simple*. No empirical cloudiness can be allowed to affect it.—It must rather be of the purest crystal. But this crystal does not appear as an abstraction, but as something concrete—indeed as the *hardest* thing there is. (PI, sec. 97, condensed)

We break the hypnotic spell of that *idée fixe* by turning our attention to different ways of picturing language and logic. In the *Investigations* Wittgenstein compares language to *games* and logic to *rules*: just as there are a variety of games and a variety of ways in which playing them is regulated, so there are a variety of "language games" and a variety of ways in which the use of words is regulated. Later, in *On Certainty*, he compares the significant use of words to a stream guided in its flow by banks and a river bed:

> And the bank of that river consists partly of hard rock, subject to no alteration or only to an imperceptible one, partly of sand, which now in one place now in another gets washed away, or deposited./ [And] the river bed of thoughts may shift. But I distinguish between the movement of the waters on the river bed and

---

36. *TLP*, 4–4.002 and 6–6.001. See Schulte's *Wittgenstein*, pp. 56–57 for an explanation of the symbols.

> the shift of the bed itself; though there is not a *sharp* division of the
> one from the other. (OC, secs. 99 and 97, my emphasis)

That an earthen channel subjected to an unaccustomed rush of water may become part of the flow it used to contain does not imply that a *real* channel would be made of *super*-hard material. That a steel rod used today to measure things may tomorrow be measured against something still harder does not imply that ordinary measuring rods merely approximate to "a measuring rod than which none harder can be conceived."

Logic is the order existing between the concepts of language, experience, and world. But when we investigate this order, we are always tempted to look for "a *super*-order existing between *super*-concepts":

> Whereas, of course, if the words "language," "experience," "world"
> have a use, it must be as humble a one as that of the words "table,"
> "lamp," "door." (PI, sec. 97 b)

"Our real need," as philosophers investigating the logic of language, is to return from the "slippery ice" of super concepts to the "rough ground" of everyday speech. We need to take a close look at the actual use of words, and to survey it from a *logical* point of view—"as we do about the pieces in chess when we are stating the rules of the game."[37] Like games, language games are normative activities: we let ourselves be guided by their rules. Our real need in philosophy is to survey these rules that actually guide our use of words.

PHILOSOPHICAL INVESTIGATION (SECTIONS 109–133)

Philosophical investigation aims at the logical clarification of thoughts. This aim is to be achieved not by digging for what is hidden (sec. 126) but by learning to notice what is always before one's eyes (sec. 129). "Digging for what is hidden" leads, in philosophy, to what Wittgenstein calls *metaphysics*.

 "What *we* do is to bring words back from their metaphysical to their everyday use" (sec. 116 b). For example, we transform the metaphysical claim that the ego is incorporeal into the grammatical observation that the pronoun *I* cannot be substituted for descriptions of the body.[38]

"We bring words back from their metaphysical to their everyday use."[39] For example:

> The man who said one can't step twice into the same river
> [Heraclitus], said something false; one *can* step twice into the same

---

37. *PI*, sec. 108, concluded. Cf. sec. 81.
38. See *BB*, p. 74 and Brenner, *Logic*, pp. 127–131.
39. This and the other quotations in this paragraph are from the Wittgenstein *ms* called "The Early Investigations." See David G. Stern's *Wittgenstein on Mind and Language*, p. 174. (The translation is Stern's.)

river.—And sometimes an object ceases to exist when I stop looking at it, and [*pace* solipsists[40]] sometimes it doesn't.—And [*pace*
Locke[41]], sometimes we *know* which color the other sees, if he
looks at this object, and sometimes we don't.

"And this is how the solution of all philosophical difficulties looks. Our
answers, if they are to be correct, must be everyday and trivial.—For these
answers make fun of the questions, as it were."[42]

In our philosophical investigations we can avoid "ineptness or empti-
ness in our assertions only by presenting the model [e.g., a simple language
game] as . . . an object of comparison, . . . not as a preconceived idea to which
reality *must* correspond. (The dogmatism into which we fall so easily in doing
philosophy.)" An earlier version of that passage (sec. 131) continued with the
following helpful illustration:

> It is true: a unit of measurement is well chosen if it expresses many
> of the lengths that we want to measure with it in whole numbers.
> But dogmatism maintains that any length *must* be a whole multi-
> ple of our unit of measurement.[43]

What, then, is the goal of philosophical investigation and how will we
know when we have reached it? A philosophical investigation is an activity of
conceptual clarification provoked by a philosophical problem. It aims at complete clarity and is satisfied only when the philosophical problem disappears
completely. Answering the question or solving the problem is not its goal.
"Philosophy unties knots in our thinking." When it has completed its work,
we are left—not with answers to a question but simply—no knots.[44])

PROPOSITIONS AND LOGIC (SECTIONS 134–137)

"This is how things are": the *Tractatus* had puffed up these humble words into
"The General Form of the Proposition" (4.5, 6); here they are deflated—
"brought back from their metaphysical to their everyday use."

Doesn't everyone know what a proposition is? Then how is this knowledge to be expressed, if not in a formula? It is to be expressed by giving examples of various kinds of propositions, showing how other kinds can be

---

40. On solipsism, see: *TLP*, 5.62, 5.64; *WLA*, pp. 21–28; *BB*, pp. 48, 57–59, 63–64, 71;
PI, secs. 24, 402–403.
41. *Essay* II: xxxii, 15. I discuss Locke's so-called "inverted spectrum problem" in connection with *PI*, secs. 273–274.
42. If its *aim* were to produce such answers, then philosophical investigation would be
a trivial pursuit. That is *not* its aim, however. See *PI*, sec. 128.
43. From the "Early Investigations" quoted in Stern, op. cit., p. 103. Cf. *WLA*, p. 69
(quoted below on p. 87).
44. *Z*, sec. 452. Cf. Norman Malcolm, *Problems of Mind*, preface.

constructed on the analogy of these, saying that we would scarcely include this or that among propositions, and so on.[45]

Lectures on the Foundations of Mathematics describes a "nucleus" of what we call propositions and claims that the laws of logic show the technique of using them:

> [B]y "propositions" we mean such things as "It rains," "There are three chairs in the room," etc. English sentences about physical objects, sense datum propositions [about states of consciousness]: this forms the nucleus of what we call propositions;[46] and it is the practice or technique of using these expressions which is shown by the laws of logic./ [For example:] if we said, "The law of contradiction doesn't hold" or "'Not both p and not p' is no longer true," we would be saying that we are not using "not" and "and" as negation and conjunction any more, or that "p" is not a proposition, or something of the sort.—Thus we might say that the laws of logic show what we do with propositions, as opposed to expressing opinions or convictions.
>
> They are not unique in this. . . . / [For example,] we might call a propositions like "There is no reddish green" a law of thought. . . .
>
> What would go wrong if we denied these laws? Nothing: except that it would upset our system. And that means simply upsetting *us*. For it doesn't mean that there is no longer any system.[47]

Adding "reddish green" to the series "reddish blue," "reddish yellow," etc. would upset our system of color terms. We have no use for it there nor (for various reasons) are we inclined to change our system and *give* it a use. And so we rule it out of our language.[48]

Following a Rule
(Sections 138–242)

"Following according to the rule is FUNDAMENTAL to our language game. It characterizes what we call description" (*RFM*, p. 330). "The rule-gov-

---

45. Compare *PI*, sec. 75. Secs. 67–69 are also relevant.
46. Just as integers and fractions form the nucleus of what we call "numbers," so sentences about physical objects and states of consciousness form the nucleus of what we call "propositions." (Cf. *PI*, secs. 67–68.) Wittgenstein's talk of a "nucleus" is reminiscent of Aristotle on "*pros hen* predication"—e.g., that "healthy" is said of an organism primarily and of a diet and complexion secondarily, in relation to health in the organism. (I say a bit more about this in *Logic and Philosophy*, pp. 26–27.)
47. *LFM*, pp. 231–232 and 235. Compare *Z*, sec. 372.
48. For more on the logic of color terms, see "Color Grammar," below.

erned nature of our languages permeates our life" (*RC*, p. 57). But what are rules? What is it for language to be rule governed?

UNDERSTANDING A WORD (SECTIONS 138–142)

What comes before our minds when we understand a word? Suppose that when we hear the word *cube* the same image of a cube comes before both our minds, but that *I* go on to apply it to a cube while you go on to apply it to a triangular prism. Shall we say that the word *cube* has the same meaning both times? If we say no to that, should we not also say no to the idea that the meaning of a word is something that comes before the mind when we understand it?

There is always more than one imaginable way to apply a picture, pattern, or paradigm. If we believe a particular application *forces* itself on us, does this belief amount to any more than that only the one application *occurred* to us?

UNDERSTANDING A SERIES (SECTIONS 143–150)

Imagine a language game of order and obedience in which a child is asked to write down a series of numbers in decimal notation. How does he come to understand this notation? Perhaps we will at first guide his hand in writing out the series "0 to 9." If we cannot get him to go on and write it down independently and in the right order, then his capacity to learn may have come to an end. The effect of any further explanation we give will depend on his reaction.[49]

Suppose the pupil finally continues the series correctly—i.e., in accord with established practice. Would we then have the right to say that he understands it? Yes, if he is often successful; no, if he does it right once in a hundred attempts. *Objection*: To have understood the system can't consist in continuing the series up to the hundredth place or even beyond: that's just *applying* one's understanding.[50] *Reply*: What does the understanding grasp that enables it to generate the series? If you say "a formula, or something like a formula," then recall that we can always think of more than one application of a formula. And so application—the *way* the formula is used and the series completed—is still a criterion of understanding. *Objection*: But I can tell you from my own personal experience that I know how to apply the formula quite apart from remembering actual applications to particular numbers. *Reply*: What is this knowledge of yours? If it is simply your ability to apply the formula correctly, then that personal experience cannot assure you that your knowledge is genuine—you will have to go by the same criterion as other people: your performance record. *Objection*: I want to say that my knowledge of the series con-

49. Compare *BB*, p. 93 (# 30) and pp. 104–105 (# 50).
50. Compare *BB*, p. 143.

sists in a certain *state of mind* by means of which the manifestations of that knowledge are explained. *Reply:* Is there an independent criterion for that "state" of yours, some way of telling that it's present—apart from observing the "manifestations" you want to explain? If not, then you need to recall the doctor in Molière who assured a patient that opium puts people to sleep because of its dormitive power. Shall we say that he has *explained* anything if he teaches us no way of testing a substance for this "power," independent of watching it put people to sleep?

"NOW I CAN GO ON!" (SECTIONS 151–155)

(A dialogue)

A: A student watches a teacher write down a series of numbers; after a while she says, "Now I understand! Now I can continue the series." What happened?

B: Various things may have happened.

A: Must there not be one essential process of understanding underneath all that variety?

B: Then do you have to *uncover* something before you can say, "Now I understand"? If so, how do you know when you find the right thing? And even if you found a process occurring uniquely in all cases of understanding, why call *it* the understanding?

A: When I utter the formula of a series with understanding, I have a particular experience. I want to say that *it* stands behind my expansion of the series. I am inclined to call that particular experience the understanding.

B: What you experienced occurred in the course of mathematical instruction. Wasn't it that particular context that "stood behind" your claim to have understood the formula? Wasn't your inclination to call that particular experience "understanding the formula" traceable to those particular circumstances?[51]

"ADD TWO" (SECTION 185)

We are back in the teaching situation described in sec. 143 and have induced our pupil to continue the "plus 2" series beyond 1000. To our chagrin, he writes 1000, 1004, 1008, 1012. We say: "Look how you began the series! You were meant to go on in the same way." If he answered, pointing to the series,

---

51. Sections 156–184 interpolate an investigation of reading and a comparison of "knowing how to read" with "knowing how to go on." I think the first-time reader should jump over these rich and interesting sections, in the interest of not obscuring the woods for the trees.

that he *did* go on in the same way, it would be of no use to repeat the old examples and explanations. Here we might speak of an abnormal reaction to our instruction. Compare reacting to a pointing gesture by looking from finger tip to wrist.

Remarking in a 1939 lecture that it is an "immensely important fact about human beings" that we react to the pointing gesture in a particular way, Wittgenstein told the following charming and instructive Story of Boo:

> If you have learned a technique of language, and I point to this coat and say to you, "The tailors now call this color 'boo'" then you will buy me a coat of this color, fetch one, etc. The point is that one only has to point to something and say "This is so-and-so" and everyone who has been through a certain preliminary training will react in the same way. We could imagine this not to happen. If I just say, "This is called 'boo,'" you might not know what I mean; but in fact you would all of you automatically follow certain rules.
>
> Ought we to say that you would follow the *right* rule?—that you would know *the* meaning of "boo"? No, clearly not. For which meaning? Are there not 10,000 meanings which "boo" might now have?—It sounds as if your learning how to use it were different from your knowing its meaning. *But the point is that we all make the SAME use of it.* To know its meaning is to use it *in the same way* as other people do.
>
> You might say, "Isn't there something else too? Something besides the agreement? Isn't there a *more natural* and a *less natural* way of behaving? . . . Suppose the word "color" [is] used as it is now used in English. "Boo" is a new word. But then we are told, "This color is called 'boo,'" and then everyone uses it for a shape. Could I then say, "That's not the straight way of using it"? I should certainly say that they behaved unnaturally.
>
> This hangs together with the question of how to continue the series of cardinal numbers. Is there a criterion for the continuation—for a right and a wrong way—except that we do in fact continue them in that way, apart from a few cranks who can be neglected? (LFM, pp. 182-183)

"How do You Mean?" (Sections 186–190)

A: What determines the step the pupil should take at any particular stage of carrying out the order "Add 2"?

B: He should do what accords with the order—as the teacher meant it. The pupil who continued the series after 1000 with "1004, 1008, 1012" didn't do as the teacher intended. For she meant, of course, that he should write "1002."

A: Your words conjure up the picture of an act of meaning mysteriously traversing an infinity of possible steps. Why not say that the steps are determined by the algebraic formula—and leave it at that?

B: What do you mean by saying that the formula determines the steps? Are you making an anthropological point about how normal people react to a certain training, or a mathematical point about the kind of formula involved?

A: It's the way the formula is *meant* that determines the steps to be taken!

B: But how do we know the way a particular formula is meant? Isn't it because we've been trained in the use of such formulas and understand their customary use? When, in particular cases, we are in doubt, we ask the teacher for clarification.

SIGNALLING (SECTIONS 194C–196)

A: When I understand the meaning of a word or a formula, the future use is in some sense already present.

B: How queer that an act taking place now can contain the future—which, of course, does not now exist!

A: Our talk of suddenly understanding sounds queer only when we misconstrue it as describing a queer process. If we think of it instead as a signalling of one's readiness to go on in the task of applying the word or formula, then it does not sound queer.

B: How then is the "readiness" one signals connected with one's future performance?

A: If you don't actually go on to perform in a certain way, then your signal was a "false start" and you didn't really understand. This is a rule of the language game in which we say things such as "Now I get it!" It is this rule—not some mysterious process—that supplies the connection. (Compare philosophical puzzlement about "suddenly understanding" with a child's surprise at hearing that a tailor can "sew a dress." He thought this meant that a dress was produced by sewing one thread on to another!)

"WHAT'S A LIST OF RULES TO ME?" (SECTIONS 197–201)

A: Chess is the game it is because of its rules. But I am not thinking of its rules when I express a wish to play it. So where is the connection between the rules and my wish?

B: The connection is not to be found in something going on in your mind (or brain) when you say, "Let's play a game of chess"; it is to be found in the day-to-day practice of playing the game and in the list of rules used in teaching it.

A: What does a list of rules have to do with my actions?

B: Just as a person can go by signposts only insofar as there exists an established way of using them (a custom), so a person can go by a list of rules only insofar as there exists a customary, established use of such lists.

A: But I don't see how a rule shows me what I must do at any particular point. For it seems that *anything* I do might be interpreted as accord with the rule.

B: It is only against a background of established practice that we can speak of accord or conflict with rules. So whether your action accords or conflicts with the rule is a matter not of any interpretation you can give, but of whether it exhibits what we call "obeying the rule" or "going against it" in practice.

FOLLOWING A RULE IS A PRACTICE (SECTIONS 202–205)

Imagine that one of a pair of chimpanzees once scratched the figure " | - - | " in the earth and thereupon the other scratched " | - - | | - - | | - - | | - - | ":

> [T]he first would not have given a rule nor would the other be following it, whatever else went on at the same time in the mind of the two of them.
>
> If however there were observed, e.g., the phenomenon of a kind of instruction, of showing how and of imitation, of lucky and misfiring attempts, of reward and punishment and the like; if at length the one who had been so trained put figures, which he had never seen before, one after another in sequence, as in the first example, then we should probably say that the one chimpanzee was writing rules down, and the other was following them. (*RFM*, p. 345)

"To obey a rule, to make a report, to give an order, to play a game of chess, are *customs* (uses, institutions)." In other words: like games (such as chess), language games (such as giving and obeying orders) are established patterns of (correct or incorrect) behavior. Just as understanding a move in chess implies knowing how to play the game, so understanding a sentence in a language implies knowing how to speak the language.

To understand a language is to be master of a technique, or multiplicity of techniques.[52] And to be master of a technique is to be guided by rules.

---

52. *Nota bene*: Although language learning must *begin* with mastering certain techniques, it need not *end* there. See *PI*, p. 216 ("secondary sense") and p. 227 ("expert judgment"). Compare pp. 144–145 ("Using Words in a Secondary Sense"), below.

If it were possible to obey a rule "privately," i.e., apart from a background of established practice, then *thinking* one was obeying a rule would be the same as obeying it.

Objection: I might invent a game that never gets played. *Reply*: That makes sense only because there's an institution (custom, practice, technique) of making up games and playing them. *Objection*: You forget about the mental process of intention! The existence of a custom is not necessary to *it*. Thus two people might begin to play a game of chess in a world in which otherwise no games exist—if only they intend to do so. *Reply*: Chess is defined by its rules. It makes sense to speak of the presence of these rules in the mind of the person intending to play chess only against the background of an established practice of teaching and playing the game.

FOLLOWING A RULE IS LIKE . . . (SECTIONS 206–223)

A: We react to rules in a particular way and were trained to do so. Following rules is like obeying the orders of someone we respect or fear.

B: Suppose different people react in different ways to the same order and training. Who is right?

A: If there is an established practice among these people ("a custom"), then "the right way" will mean "the customary way."[53]

B: Suppose you travel to a strange country with an unknown language. In what circumstances would you say the people there give, obey, and rebel against orders?

A: Common human behavior is the system of reference by which we interpret an unknown language—a point vividly illustrated in the following reflections on an imaginary encounter with two spherical creatures:

> If one [of them] emits a scream and continues to scream until the other rolls toward it, then we could interpret this screaming as the expression of a wish or craving. If . . . instead of a scream we were to witness the appearance of a red patch on one of the creatures which also continued until its companion rolled toward it, then we should hardly be justified in thus interpreting its conduct, and all resemblance to what we ourselves call signs would have disappeared. To attempt an interpretation under these circumstances

---

53. Recall the example in sec. 145 of a pupil leaning how to continue a series: " [L]et us suppose that after some efforts on the teacher's part he continues the series correctly, that is, as we do it. So now we can say he has mastered the system."

would be as pointless as to refer to the expression of a shelf or the attitude of a wall.[54]

B: Let's return to human beings. Suppose we encounter people in an unknown country who carry on the usual human activities and in the course of them seem to employ an articulate language. Won't we say they are speaking a language?

A: Suppose we can find no regular connection between the sounds these people make and their actions, so that we are unable to "get the hang" of what they are doing.[55] Are we still to say they have a *language*: orders, rules, and the rest? There's not enough regularity for us to call it that.

B: Do you want to explain "rule" (*Regel*) by means of "regularity" (*Regelmäßigkeit*)?

A: I want to say: those words are learned together, not one by means of the other. They are learned by example and practice—in the course, for instance, of learning how to continue an ornamental pattern uniformly when told to do so.

B: Doesn't the learner have to reach beyond all the examples and explanations you can give him? Won't he have to guess at how you mean them to be taken?[56]

A: He usually understands them without needing to guess at how I mean them. When he doesn't, he may then think up various interpretations and guess at one of them.

B: Any instruction you give him can be variously interpreted. So how does he know how to proceed in any given case?

A: If by "How does he know?" you mean, "Does he have reasons?," the answer is that his reasons will soon give out—then he will act, without reasons.

---

54. Friedrich Waismann, *Principles of Linguistic Philosophy*, p. 110. This book was to be a textbook of Wittgenstein's philosophy. Wittgenstein collaborated with Waismann on it for a time.

55. These people don't seem to be playing language *games*. Compare *PI*, sec. 23: "Here the term 'language *game*' is meant to bring into prominence the fact that the *speaking* of language is part of . . . a form of life." Cf. *PI*, sec. 237, and below, "Sensations, Beetles," pp. 96–98.

56. Compare with how (according to *PI*, sec. 32) Augustine thought a child learns his mother tongue.

And if he acts in such-and-such a way, we will say he has understood us and mastered the technique we wanted to teach.

B: Doesn't the lack of reasons bother you?

A: Not always. Not when I'm ordered to continue a familiar pattern by someone I respect or fear!

B: But the initial segment of even the simplest series can be variously interpreted.

A: It can in the abstract; it cannot in such-and-such particular circumstances.

"Rule," "Agreement," "Same" (Sections 224–228)

These words are interwoven in our everyday use of them. And as we learn new language games, we learn new uses of "same and different," "agreement and disagreement." We learn a whole family of contrasts.

The Compass User (Sections 229–237)

Imagine someone carrying one point of a compass along a fixed line while using the other point to draw a new line. As he draws it, he alters the opening of his compass while he looks intently at the fixed line as if following it. If we are unable to learn a technique of following the fixed line by watching him, we will conclude that he is not really being guided by it. His behavior looks like rule following without being rule following. (We may suggest that he is hearkening to an inspiration—which would imply he is not following a rule. Or we may compare him to a preschooler making up a story while looking at a printed page and imitating the reading behavior of adults.)[57]

Can a Rule Contain All its Applications? (Section 238–239)

A: It's as if a rule produced all its consequences in advance.

B: The phenomenon you describe reflects the fact that we draw its consequences as a matter of course. If told to go to the store and buy gumdrops of various colors, we will apply our basic color vocabulary as a matter of course—without reflection and interpretation.

A: Don't we sometimes justify our description of a thing's color by comparing it to the color of a standard sample?

B: Yes, but justifications come to an end. Then I'm inclined to say: "That's simply what I do." What I do exhibits my knowhow, shows I'm master of a technique.

---

57. Cf. secs. 207, 269, and 653.

A: When I call the color of the sky "blue," I justify that to myself by making sure what I see matches my mental image of blue. That's my criterion.

B: How do you know the image you call up is really an image of *blue?* By matching it with yet another image? (Consider the order "*imagine* a red patch." Are you tempted in this case to think that before *obeying* you must have imagined a red patch to serve as your pattern?. . . [58])

AGREEMENT (SECTIONS 240–242)

Disputes do not normally break out over the application of basic color, number, and shape predicates. Here there reigns a nearly complete harmony in the application of words. This harmony is part of the framework on which the working of our language is based. For at this basic level, understanding a language just *is* mastery of a technique:

> We say: if a child has mastered language—and hence its application —it must know the meaning of words. It must, for example, be able to attach the name of its color to a white, black, red or blue object without the occurrence of any doubt. And indeed no one misses doubt here. . . . (OC, secs. 522–523)

This precritical "mastery of a technique" belongs to the "river bed" that channels human thought and action.[59]

As a kind of agreement or harmony between citizens is fundamental to civil society, so a kind of agreement or harmony between speakers seems fundamental to language. But we need to distinguish *agreement in opinion* from the more fundamental *agreement in language*—as in the following example:

If we share the opinion that the color of Peter's shirt is magenta, this presupposes agreement in our definition of "magenta"; If someone disagrees with our judgment, we can show her a sample from a standard color chart ("a defining sample") and ask her to compare the color of the shirt with the color of the sample. But in many other cases there would be no comparable response to disagreements. Suppose, for example, that someone objects to saying that scarlet and pink are shades of the same color. If he asks what they have in common that entitles us to call them shades of the same color, could we show

---

58. BB, p. 3, paraphrased. Cf. *RFM*, p. 333: "To what extent can the function of a rule be described? Someone who is master of none, I can only train. But how can I explain the nature of a rule to myself? The difficulty here is not, to dig down to the ground; no, it is to recognize the ground that lies before us as ground."

59. The river bed image comes from *OC*, secs. 94–99. Cf. Toulmin, "The Marginal Relevance of Theory in the Humanities."

him? No. We would reject his request for a demonstration by saying "Don't you *see?*"[60]

The "Don't you see?" response is an appeal to agreement in judgment (or "agreement in reaction," as Wittgenstein also calls it); it reminds us that people just *do* see (react to) certain things as "the same" in such cases.[61] Without this sort of agreement, there would be no practice of using color words to describe the appearance of objects at all. And without this practice, there would be no agreement or disagreement in opinion (e.g., over whether Peter's shirt is magenta, whether to call a color reddish blue rather than bluish red). If we did not normally agree in such elementary judgments as that fresh blood and ripe cherries are red, then there would not be enough regularity to say that the "color words" are rule-governed—i.e., that a distinction between "correct" and "incorrect judgment" had been established for them.[62]

To conclude: Communication with one another by means of language requires a certain agreement between us—an agreement not only in defini-

tions (in the rules we appeal to in explaining and justifying the use of words) but also in judgments (in our actual application of the rules). For example, we must agree not only in our ostensive definition of "red" (in what we point to in teaching the word), but also (to a large extent) in what things we go on to describe as "red."

Objection: Granted that the language game we play with "red" is a means of communication between us. I still want to say there is *another* language game—one I use in talking to myself about my innermost feelings—that is not such a means of communication.

MIND
Sensation
(through Section 315)

My sensations are private in the sense that "nobody can know them unless I show them." Are they also private in the deeper sense that I can never *really*

---

60. The preceding example is from *BB*, p. 131. Another example is on p. 140 (paraphrased): When we hear the diatonic scale, we say that after every seven notes the same note recurs. Asked *why* we call it the same, we answer "Well, it's a C again." Pressed to explain what made us call it C again, we exclaim "Don't you *hear* it's the same note, only an octave higher?" Cf. Hanfling, *Wittgenstein's Later Philosophy*, ch. 4.
61. "It is of the greatest importance that a dispute hardly ever arises between people about whether the color of this object is the same as the color of that, the length of this rod the same as the length of that, etc. This *peaceful agreement* is the characteristic surrounding of the use of the word 'same'"(*RFM*, p. 323, my emphasis).
62. Suppose we overhear people calling the clear sky "red" and glowing coals "blue." Would they be playing the language game of color judgment at all? I discuss this question in my remarks on secs. 273–280. Cf. p. 86 ff, below ("Agreement in Language").

show them at all: "I can show you the *sign*, never the feeling" (*PO*, p. 447)? It is true that in everyday speech I *can* show my feelings—show as opposed to just telling you about them (so that you can know, not just know *about* them). But it is also true that those everyday uses look problematic when we reflect on them. Why this is so, how a "deeper" use of the words might appear less problematic—these belong to the nest of questions investigated in the following sections.[63]

"THE PRIVATE LANGUAGE PROBLEM" (SECTION 243)

Is language always and necessarily communicable to another? Does it really depend for its possibility on "agreement in reactions"? Can we not imagine a language game with words that refer to what can only be known to the individual speaking? It would be used solely for the purpose of taking stock of one's immediate private experiences; so the reactions of others would seem to be irrelevant.

HOW "PAIN" REFERS TO PAIN (SECTIONS 244–257)

How do the words *pain, tingle,* and *itch* actually come to refer to (name, signify) a person's sensations? *Not* in the way *slab, pillar,* and *beam* come to refer to building stones. You will recall that the builder taught his assistant the names of building stones with the help of "ostensive training." There is nothing comparable in the way adults teach children the names of sensations.

"Pain is something *inner.* That's why adults *can't* teach their children 'pain' ostensively": this, like other philosophical explanations, is best regarded as an effort to state a rule of language. The point is that if words could be learned in the way words for "outer objects" are learned, they would not, by that very fact, signify what we call *sensations.*[64]

So how *do* words come to refer to sensations? One possibility is that they are connected with the natural, prelinguistic expressions of the sensation and used in their place. Thus, a child hurts himself and cries; then adults talk to him and teach him exclamations and, later, sentences. They teach him new pain behavior.

So if human beings showed no outward signs of pain, it would not be possible to teach children the use of the word *pain. Objection:* What if the child is a genius and himself invents a name for the sensation? *Reply:*

> [I]n order to establish a name relation we have to establish a technique of use. And we are misled if we think that it is a peculiar

---

63. Perhaps this "deeper privacy" should be counted among the "super-concepts" we were warned against in *PI*, sec. 97.

64. The manuscript passage from which *PI*, sec. 248 was culled is relevant here. See Stern, p. 186.

process of christening an object which makes a word the word for an object. This is a kind of superstition. So it's no use saying that we have a private object before the mind and give it a name. There is a name only where there is a technique of using it. That technique *can* be private; but this only means that nobody but I know about it. I might have a sewing machine that nobody else knows about. But in order to be a *private* sewing machine, it must be an object which deserves the name "sewing machine." And it would deserve that name not in virtue of its privacy but in virtue of its similarity to other sewing machines, private or otherwise.[65]

The S-Game (Sections 258–264)

Section 258, commonly known as "the private language argument" or "diary passage," is among the most famous short texts in recent philosophy. Here it is, paraphrased and in the form of a dialogue between the would-be diarist *D* and a questioner, *Q*:

D: I want to keep a diary about the recurrence of a certain sensation; to that end I associate it with the sign "S" and write this sign in a diary for every day on which I have the sensation.

Q: Then a definition of "S" cannot be formulated.

D: I can give myself a kind of ostensive definition.

Q: But how does one point to a sensation?

D: I write down "S" and at the same time I concentrate my attention on the sensation—and so, as it were, point to it inwardly.

Q: That sounds more like an idle ceremony than a definition. A definition must establish the meaning of a sign.

D: I did that when I concentrated my attention; for I thereby impressed on myself the connection between the sign and the sensation.

Q: What does that mean?

D: It means that I brought it about that I remember the connection *correctly* in the future.

Q: Then what is your criterion of correctness?

D: I want to say that whatever is going to seem right to me here *is* right.

Q: But then we can't talk about right anymore.[66]

---

65. From "Notes for the 'Philosophical Lecture,'" *PO*, p. 448. I have modified the wording a bit in hopes of improving its intelligibility.

66. My dialogue format for sec. 258 is adapted from Oswald Hanfling, *Language and the Privacy of Experience*, pp. 18–19.

Drawing now on material from secs. 259–264, I imagine the following continuation of the preceding dialogue:

Q: Remind me of what you mean by "S."

D: A certain sensation.

Q: What sensation?

D: I can't remind you of that because it's not the kind of thing you ever knew, or could ever know. I can, of course, remind myself. I simply call up my memory image of the sensation I originally named "S." I use that image as a paradigm: I call any sensation that matches it "S."

Q: How did you know which image to call up?

D: I'm known for my good memory!

Q: The point is: you were trying to recall what "S" means by calling up an image. But you couldn't have known *which* image to recall unless you *already* remembered what S means.

D: I just knew it was the right one!

Q: Then what do you mean by "the right image"?

D: The memory image of S, of course.

Q: You can't identify the image as an image of S unless "S" *already* has a meaning. But the image was supposed to be the paradigm in terms of which you defined "S" for yourself.

D: Here I want to say that whatever seems to me right *is* right.

Q: Then you're not really talking about "right"!

D: Compare "S" with "pain." What gives any of us the right to speak of correctly or incorrectly using *that* word?

Q: We say that "pain" is being used correctly, rightly, only if the speaker uses it "in accordance with the usual symptoms and presuppositions of pain" (*PI*, sec. 271). If she regularly uses it in circumstances in which everybody else would use the word "tired" (for example), then she would be using it wrongly and we would conclude that she doesn't know what the word means.

D: I write "S" only when I feel that my present sensation is the *same* as that to which I previously gave that name.

Q: That shows only that your present sensation is accompanied by a certain *impression*—one you express by saying, "It's the same!" But to express an impression is not to give meaning to a word.

D: I *believe* I have S again!

Q: That presupposes the very point I've been questioning: that you ever succeeded in making "S" into the name of a sensation.

D: I certainly have *something* when I write down "S" in my diary!

Q: If my banker, without context or explanation, were to say, "I have something," I might react by asking: "Is it money, debts, or an empty safe?"[67]

Contrast the diarist's S-game of sec. 258 with the builder's language of sec. 2. *It*, the S-game, is a parasitic or "secondary" use of language and so could not be conceived as "the *whole* language of a tribe" (sec. 6). When the diarist said he gave a name to his sensation, he forgot "that a great deal of stage-setting in the language is presupposed if the mere act of naming is to make sense" (sec. 257). It makes sense to say that someone has given a name to a sensation only if we can assume that he knows what a sensation *is*; but we can do that only if we can assume that in general he uses the language of sensations correctly.

We saw an enlargement of the builder's language in sec. 8. Numerals, demonstratives, and color samples were added to the original set of building-stone names:

> A [the builder] gives an order like: "d–slab–there." At the same time he shows the assistant [B] a color sample, and when he says "there" he points to a place on the building site. From the stock of slabs B takes one for each letter of the alphabet up to "d," of the same color as the color sample, and brings them to the place indicated by A. (*PI*, sec. 8)

Is the sensation the diarist "points to inwardly" analogous to the builder's color sample? No, because a sensation (impression, or mental image) lacks the objectivity that makes it possible for color samples (among other things) to function as paradigms or standards of comparison.

In the story quoted earlier, a certain tailor points to a patch of cloth and says, "boo."[68] He doesn't call it "boo" because it *is* boo; it's "boo" because he *calls* it that. He is teaching his assistants a new color word of his own invention. Then he can order them to go to the store and buy boo-colored cloth. He

---

67. Compare *PI*, sec. 294.
68. See my comments on *PI*, sec. 185 (pp. 34–35, above).

will be able to check whether they have obeyed an order by comparing the cloth they bring back with the patch he pointed to when he defined "boo." For that patch now has a paradigmatic, normative function in the language game. And so it is no longer the tailor's calling it "boo" that makes it boo: he may be pointing to the wrong patch of cloth; he may be mistaking the "blue" for the "boo" paradigm because of bad lighting or the like.

The diarist claims to be using the sensation he had "pointed to inwardly" as a paradigm: whenever another sensation occurs, he compares it with that. "But what if he points to the wrong thing?" Here the question of right or wrong has no application. The diarist cannot be making a mistake about his "paradigm": he judges it, not it him. It has no normative function: it is the mere impression of a rule.

"PRIVATE JUSTIFICATION" (SECTIONS 265–266)

A: We sometimes justify things by appeal to a table. Why not also call it justification if the table is to be looked up only in the imagination? Why not call it "private justification"?

B: What is "looking up a word in the imagination" supposed to mean?

A: When I'm unsure of my memory of the train's departure time, it sometimes helps to recall how the page of the timetable looked. Isn't it the same with our "private diarist"? Can't he (as it were) look up a sample of sensation S in the dictionary of his memory?

B: If you describe what you say you recalled when you wanted to remember the departure time of the train, we may have to conclude that you recalled the wrong thing—e.g., the *airplane* schedule. If the diarist "consults the dictionary of his memory," he is engaging in an idle ceremony: to him "whatever is going to seem right is right." And so the cases are not parallel. (For really parallel cases, compare the diarist of sec. 258 with the clock watcher of sec. 266 who stares at a clock and moves its hands until their position strike him as right. And compare both with the compass user of sec. 237.)

THE "INVERTED SPECTRUM" OBJECTION (SECTIONS 273–280)

O: Is there *no* subjective side to the meaning of everyday language? Take color words. Objectively speaking it is right to call the clear sky blue: it fits with what other people say. But what about *my* experience—the experience I have when looking at what everybody calls blue? I certainly know how the color looks to me; so I can have a private word to stand for that—a word with a purely subjective meaning. Doesn't that make sense?

R: What sense? If I were asked how the color blue looks to me, I would say "cool."

O: That's not the sort of thing I mean! When I say I know how the color looks to me, I mean that I can point inwardly and say, "It looks like *this*."

R: One doesn't define a criterion of identity by emphatic stressing of the word "this"![69]

HUMAN BEHAVIOR (SECTIONS 281–282)

Do you mean that whenever we feel pain we must somehow express it? No. The point is that expression is part of the very concept of pain. In other words: it makes sense to apply this concept only to creatures capable of expressing pain in their behavior; even when we do not express our pain, we remain the kind of creatures for whom certain ways of expressing it are normal.

We do sometimes say of inanimate things, "They're in pain": when playing with dolls for instance. But that is a *secondary* application of the concept of pain. People who ascribed pain *only* to dolls (where there is no pain behavior) would not be operating with the same concept.

MIND/BODY (SECTION 286)

A: Is it the body that feels pain, or the mind?

B: If you tell me you have a sore hand, aren't you telling me about part of your body?

C: The pain is correctly said to be in the hand; yet it is not the *hand* that utters the sounds. Nor is it to the hand, or to the mouth, that we address comforting remarks, but to the sufferer. And what we look at when we offer comfort is the sufferer's eyes—though we don't imagine he feels pain there. Given this complexity, we distort our concept of pain if we treat pain as a "something" that's either in one thing ("the mind") or in another ("the body"). It is not a body (or part of a body) that has a pain, nor a mind, nor a bit of each: it is a living human being. The concept of pain thus cuts across the dualistic mind/body metaphysics of Descartes and his many followers.

A: Is it the mind that thinks, or the brain?

C: Why analyze everything we say of persons into statements about other things, whatever they are?[70] (We're not that hard up for categories.)

---

69. I have more to say about the problem touched on in this section ("the inverted spectrum problem") in the concluding section of "Sensations, Beetles, and 'Private Language,'" below. Cf. Hanfling, *Wittgenstein's Later Philosophy*, pp. 100–102.

70. See pp. 68–69 of Hanfling, *Language and the Privacy of Experience* (an Open University coursebook to which I am much indebted). Also relevant are Malcolm's *Problems of Mind*, pp. 73–79, and Cook's "Human Beings" (in Winch, ed., *Studies in the Philosophy of Wittgenstein*).

WITHOUT JUSTIFICATION—⫲► WITHOUT RIGHT (SECTION 289)

A: Although others may not believe me when I tell them I'm in pain, I am at any rate justified before myself.

B: What do you mean?

A: I mean that if others could know what I am calling "pain," they would admit I was using the word correctly.

B: Then I wonder what, if anything, you would call "others knowing what I'm calling 'pain'"; so I am still in the dark.

C (addressing A): Your talk of being "justified before yourself" sounds idle. For the point is not that you somehow justified the use of the word, but that you were using it "in a way fitting in with the usual symptoms and presuppositions of pain."[71]

A: I don't go by "the usual symptoms"—pain behavior—when I say, "I'm in pain"!

C: You go by *no* criterion, no identification rule, when expressing your pain.

A: Then what guides me in my use of the word *pain*?

C: If you started to use it incorrectly, i.e., out of line with "the usual symptoms and presuppositions of pain," other people would soon set you straight!

EXPRESSION/DESCRIPTION (SECTIONS 290–292)

A: When I say "I'm in pain," I'm expressing something, not identifying something. My sentence is functioning simply as a conventional replacement of a natural expression of pain such as crying. I might just as well have said, "Ouch!"[72]

B: Do you want to say that the word *pain* really means crying?

A: I want to say that the verbal expression of pain *replaces* crying, not that it describes it. If I were describing a sensation when I said, "I'm in pain," then I would be "identifying my sensation by criteria" (sec. 290); but to do that would be "trying to use language to get between pain and its expression" (sec. 245)—which would imply the wrong picture, namely:

---

71. A phrase from sec. 271. Cf. sec. 357.
72. This and the following two lines are based on sec. 244.

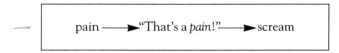

The right picture would be more like:

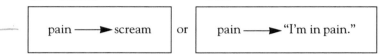

B: That's certainly not the end of the matter!

A: But it is the beginning.

B: When I truthfully tell you, "I'm in pain," my words are describing a fact. Isn't that the beginning of the language game with "pain"?

A: Don't think you're always *guided* by something when you say something meaningful:

> Don't always think that you read off what you say from the facts; that you portray these in words according to rules. For even so you would have to apply the rule in the particular case without guidance. (sec. 292; cf. sec. 201)

THE OBJECT-DESIGNATION MODEL (SECTION 293)

If "pain" functioned like the diarist's "S," there would be no room in our language for asking whether it is being used to name the right object. For example, there would be no room for asking whether what someone calls "pain" really is that kind of object—a certain sensation. But there *is* room—a newcomer to the language might confuse "pain" with one of the color words, for example. Therefore, everyday sensation words do not function in the way the diarist thinks they must, namely to name (designate, label) something one "points to inwardly."

I am reminded here of the following lines from *Remarks on the Philosophy of Psychology*:

> When one learns to use the word "pain," that does not happen through guessing which of the inner processes connected with falling down, etc. this word is used for./ For in that case this problem might arise as well: on account of *which* of my sensations do I cry out when I damage myself? (*RPP* I, sec. 305)

But the "problem" alluded to is just nonsense. And that is what "construing the grammar of the expression of sensation on the model of 'object and designation'" actually comes to.[73]

---

73. For more on these matters, see my "Sensations, Beetles" essay, below.

"If we construe the grammar of the expression of sensation on the model of 'object and designation', the object drops out as irrelevant." But the object—the sensation—is not irrelevant. Talking about our pains and titillations is an important part of our lives. We need to give up, not that talk, but that philosophical way of construing it.

We need to attend to the differences between sensation words and words to which the object-designation model actually applies. For instance: "She said she (herself) had an x but was mistaken" makes sense when x is replaced by the name of a building stone, not when it is replaced by the name of a sensation. And again: "I wonder if it's really my x?" makes sense when x equals "red apple," not when it equals "throbbing pain."

"ONLY FROM MY OWN CASE" (SECTIONS 295–303)

A: I know what "pain" means only from my own case.

B: You're not describing the ordinary use of the word!

A: Our mother tongue certainly does allows us at times to say that we know someone else is in pain. But isn't this an example of the lax and arbitrary side of her nature?

B: Can you doubt, in a real case, someone else's pain or fear? Suppose you saw a child fall, cut herself, and weep, and you reacted with the words "I don't *know* she's in pain": *that* would be arbitrary!

A: *Something* accompanies my cry of pain (sec. 296); you keep talking about linguistic externals and neglect that.

B: I agree of course that pain signifies a sensation—not a piece of behavior, linguistic or otherwise.

A: Can't we get beyond that purely grammatical point? Picture two steaming kettles, both made of clear glass: one with water boiling inside it, the other without. Can't we understand "pain behavior with pain" and "pain behavior without pain" on that model?

B: Contrast your picture of water boiling in a transparent kettle with the picture of a newborn baby crying in agony. We would have to point out successively the two elements of the picture in order to explain both "boiling water" and "steaming." But we could explain both "crying" and "pain" by reference to the crying newborn without successively pointing to different elements of the picture.[74]

---

74. Based on *PI*, secs. 300–301. It does not affect the point that—like any explanations of meaning—these ostensive definitions could be variously interpreted. See secs. 26 and 28.

A: Then I'll just drop the analogy. I'll just look within myself and concentrate on my sensation. *This*, I want to say, is the important thing (sec. 298).

B: Do you also want to say, "It's exactly *this* intense," as you concentrate
on your pain?

A: Yes!

B: But are you saying anything—even to yourself—as you say that?[75]
(Does the solipsist say anything when he pronounces the words "Only I feel
real pain"? Or is it just that he is irresistibly inclined to use that form of words
and exclude other apparently analogous forms?[76])

BEHAVIORISM? (SECTIONS 300–309)

In the following cartoons, B represents behaviorism, A its opposite, dualism.
Both positions force our talk about pain into the "object-designation model"
and thereby misrepresent its grammar. (The beetle is the private diarist's inexpressible "inner something.")[77]

A   B

A		B	
Pain as distinct from behavior		Pain as distinct from behavior	(nothing)
Pain behavior		Pain behavior (= pain)	

75. Based on Z, sec. 256. Cf. "Sensations, Beetles, and 'Private Language,'" below.

76. See BB, pp. 59–60 for more on the solipsist.

77. The cartoons are from Hanfling's *Language and the Privacy of Experience*, pp. 66–67.
Used with the kind permission of the Open University.

Thought
(Sections 316 to the end of Part I)

"Thought," "understanding," "belief," "hope," "expectation," and "intention" are prominent among the concepts of mind discussed in this long stretch of the *Investigations*. Though differing among themselves in important ways, they are alike in that none are sensations. They lack the "genuine duration" (beginning, middle, end) and degree (barely perceptible to unendurable) that characterizes pain and other sensations.[78]

EXPRESSING A THOUGHT (SECTION 317)

"In a proposition a thought finds an expression that can be perceived by the senses" (*TLP*, 3.1). It would be misleading, however, to compare an expression of a thought, such as the proposition "It's raining," with an expression of pain, such as a cry. "For if I say, 'It's raining,' I don't generally want the other person to reply, 'So *that's* how it seems to *you*.' 'We're talking about the weather,' I could say, 'not about me.'"[79]

THINKING AND SPEAKING (SECTIONS 327–343)

We can certainly speak without thinking. Can we also think without speaking? (sec. 327) While making various measurements I might act in such a way that onlookers would judge that—wordlessly—I had the thought: "Two magnitudes equal to a third are equal to each other"; and it would be natural to call that "thought without speech" (sec. 330).

"So you really wanted to say . . . ": distinguish the *use* of that phrase from the *picture* it evokes. It is used to lead someone from one form of expression to another; the picture evoked is of something present in the mind waiting to be expressed. The picture "papers over" the variety of things that may persuade us to exchange one form of expression for another (sec. 334).

What happens when I try to find the right expression for my thoughts? No *one* thing: I might surrender to a mood, for example, or try to describe a picture that occurs to me. Perhaps a German sentence occurs to me and I try to hit on the corresponding sentence in English (sec. 335).

"You intended the whole sentence before you spoke it out; so it must have already existed in your mind." If I am to intend the construction of an English sentence in advance, then I must be able to speak English. Compare

78. Based on Z, sec. 472. (Cf. Z, sec. 96: "The concept 'thinking' is not a concept of an experience. For we don't compare thoughts in the same way as we compare experiences.") See Z, secs. 45, 78, 81–83, 478, 485, 488, and 624 for more on "genuine duration."
79. From Manuscript 229, quoted in Hallett's *Companion*, p. 389.

speaking a language with playing a game: if the technique of playing it did not exist, then I could not, of course, *intend* to play it (sec. 337).

"We do not equate thinking with speaking or any other corporeal process. So why not call it an *incorporeal* process?" Because that would make the difference between them seem too slight. The radical difference between another; the picture evoked is of something present in the mind waiting to be expressed. The picture "papers over" the variety of things that may persuade us to exchange one form of expression for another (sec. 334).

What happens when I try to find the right expression for my thoughts? No *one* thing: I might surrender to a mood, for example, or try to describe a picture that occurs to me. Perhaps a German sentence occurs to me and I try to hit on the corresponding sentence in English (sec. 335).

"You intended the whole sentence before you spoke it out; so it must have already existed in your mind." If I am to intend the construction of an English sentence in advance, then I must be able to speak English. Compare speaking a language with playing a game: if the technique of playing it did not exist, then I could not, of course, *intend* to play it (sec. 337).

"We do not equate thinking with speaking or any other corporeal process. So why not call it an *incorporeal* process?" Because that would make the difference between them seem too slight. The radical difference between thinking and (for example) kicking comes out only by noticing how very differently the corresponding words function in the traffic of human life—by noticing, for instance, that there is a use in language for "imagining what does not exist" but not "kicking what does not exist." Do we really want to call "thinking" the name of any process, once we have noticed such things?

"Thinking without speech is to thinking with speech as singing without expression is to singing with expression." Do we want to identify the expressiveness of a musical performance with any process—inner or outer—that may accompany it (sec. 341)?

SOMETIMES ——/—►MIGHT ALWAYS (SECTIONS 344–352)

"We sometimes say things to ourselves. What would it be like if we never said anything to others?" We only say that people speak to themselves if, in the ordinary sense, they can speak.

"You sometimes calculate in your head. Would it be possible for everybody to *always* calculate in their heads?" We only say that someone calculates in her head if, in the ordinary sense, she can calculate. (Cf. sec. 385.)

"Although these deaf mutes have learned only a sign language, perhaps each talks to himself inwardly in a vocal language." I don't know whether to say I understand that or not! (secs. 348–349).

"If I suppose that deaf mutes talk to themselves inwardly, then I am simply supposing that they do the *same* as I do when I talk to myself inwardly."

That gets us no further. It is as if I were to say: "If you know what 'It's five o'clock here' means, then you also know what 'It's five o'clock on the sun' means: namely that it is the same time there as it is here when it's five o'clock." (Sec. 350; cf. 351.)

"You *must* know what I mean when I say deaf mutes may talk to themselves inwardly!" Your words lead me to have certain images, but their usefulness goes no further. And I can also imagine something in connection with the words "five P.M. on the sun"—such as a grandfather clock that points to 5 (sec. 351).

"Although we may not *know* whether someone speaks to himself inwardly, either he *does* or he *doesn't*; there's no third possibility." What you say simply gives us a certain picture. But without an answer to the question how it is to be *applied*, the picture hangs in the air and explains nothing.[80]

MEANING AND VERIFICATION (SECTIONS 353–362)

If A hears thunder and says, "So it's raining nearby," B (overhearing him) may question his inference. But if A sees drops pouring from clouds and B accepts this fact but questions whether it is *raining*, then we would wonder whether he understands English any more. It belongs to the *sense* of certain sentences that certain criteria are applied in verifying them.

Relevant to this topic is what Wittgenstein says later about the connection between length and methods of judging length (*PI*, p. 225, a–b), and what he had said earlier, in a 1932 lecture:

> Some people say that the question, "How can one know such a thing?," is irrelevant to the question, "What is the meaning?" But an answer gives the meaning by showing the relation of the proposition to other propositions. That is, it shows what it follows from and what follows from it. It gives the grammar of the proposition . . . (*WLA*, pp. 19–20)

Verificationism? Although he is well known (if not infamous) for suggesting that theories in philosophy typically stem from conceptual confusion, some of Wittgenstein's readers are convinced that he is actually committed to the kind of idealist theory called "verificationism."[81] Wittgenstein anticipated this misunderstanding in the same 1932 lecture:

> Reading that Cambridge won the boat race, which verifies "Cambridge won," is obviously not the meaning [of the statement], but it is connected with it. . . . And if we did away with all means of verifying it, we would destroy the meaning. . . . / There is

---

80. Based on sec. 352. My commentary on secs. 514–524 is also relevant.

81. I have in mind Bernard Williams's "Wittgenstein and Idealism" (in Vesey, ed., *Understanding Wittgenstein*) and Jonathan Lear's "Leaving the World Alone" (in *Journal of Philosophy* for 1982).

a mistaken conception of my view concerning the connection between meaning and verification which turns the view into idealism. [That is into a view that would say] that *a boat race = the idea of a boat race.* The mistake here is in trying to explain something in terms of something else. . . . The difficulty with these explanations in terms of something else is that the something else may have an entirely different grammar. Consider the word "chair." If there could be no visual picture of a chair, the word would have a different meaning. That one can see a chair is essential to the meaning of the word. But a visual picture of a chair is not a chair. What would it mean to sit on the visual picture of a chair? Of course we can explain what a chair is by showing pictures of it. But that does not mean that a chair is a complex of views. (*WLA*, pp. 29–30)

Berkeley? Wittgenstein would applaud the Irish bishop's opposition to philosophers who drive a wedge between the meaning of our judgments about material ("sensible") objects and the sense experiences by which we actually verify them—philosophers such as John Locke (with his theory of an imperceptible "material substratum underlying all our sensible ideas"). But he would oppose Berkeley's verificationist analysis of material-object concepts on the grounds that it misrepresents their grammar. To Berkeley's claim that "a cherry is nothing but a congeries of sensible impressions, or ideas," Wittgenstein would respond with a question such as: "Shall we then speak of *eating* sensible impressions or ideas?"[82]

ESSENCE AND GRAMMAR (SECTIONS 365–374)

A scene in a play by Goethe opens with two characters, Adelheid and the Bishop, finishing up a game of chess. Just as they are playing a real (not a pretend) game of chess *in the play*, so we may be doing a real (not pretend) addition *in the head.*

But the words *calculating in the head* or *mental arithmetic* may seem to designate something occult, and therefore more mysterious than "playing chess in a play." What do these words really signify? What do they point to?

"What is the essence of mental arithmetic—what is it really?" This exemplifies the sort of question we encounter in philosophy: one to be decided neither by pointing to something nor by describing a process. It is a question to be decided by recalling the grammar of "doing a sum in one's head" and related phrases—their use in the language. For it was by learning how to use such phrases that we learned what mental arithmetic *is*.[83] The question,

---

82. See *Three Dialogues Between Hylas and Philonous*, p. 97. Here (but not everywhere) the Wittgensteinian reaction to Berkeley would be like Hylas's reaction to Philonous.

83. Similarly: "To know how to use the word 'anger' is to know what anger *is*" (Cavell, *The Claim of Reason*, p. 185).

"What is the essence of burning?," by contrast, *is* a question to be decided "by pointing or the description of a process"; it exemplifies the sort of essence-question *not* to be decided by recalling the use of words in the language.[84]

Why should we call "pain" the name of a sensation, "red" the name of a color? The answer lies in the normal use of these words in the language—for example, in the fact that it makes sense to predicate "red" but not "pain" of a stone or an apple. Here essence *is* decided by recalling the use of words.

"Consider: 'The only correlate in language to an intrinsic necessity is an arbitrary rule'"(sec. 372). If you talk about intrinsic necessity, you talk about essence, and

> if you talk about *essence*—, you are merely noting a convention. But here one would like to retort: there is no greater difference than that between a proposition about the depth of the essence and one about—a mere convention. But what if I reply: to the *depth* that we see in the essence there corresponds the *deep* need for the convention./ Thus [for example] if I say: "It's as if this proposition expressed the *essence* of form"—I mean: it is as if this proposition expressed a property of the entity *form*!—and one can say: the entity of which it asserts a property, and which I here call the entity "form," is the picture which I cannot help having when I hear the word "form." (*RFM*, p. 65)

"So a *convention* is all we can milk out of an intrinsic necessity into a proposition?" (*PI*, sec. 372). Avoid representing the matter as if there were something we *can't* do—as if (for example) there really were an entity called "form" whose properties we can intuit but not express.[85] Recall that in practice we can distinguish "propositions about the depth of the essence" from arbitrary conventions without reference to any such entity: "it cancels out, whatever it is "(*PI*, sec. 293).

THE IDENTITY OF IMAGES (SECTIONS 375–381)

A: Every time I pronounce the letter *a* to myself, I have a certain image. I wonder if other people have the same image when they pronounce it?

B: How do we compare images? What does "same" mean in that context?

A: The same is the same! *How* identity is verified is a purely psychological question.

---

84. Cf. *PI*, secs. 89–90.

85. For an interesting Buddhist view of these texts, see Garfield, p. 356 ("it is only conventions that bring ontology into play") and Thurman, p. 100 (on "warding off the temptation to feel disappointed with settling for conventionality"; cf. p. 92).

B: That makes no more sense than: "High is high!—whether we're talking about a tower or a musical note; it's just a matter of psychology that one sometimes *sees*, sometimes *hears* it."

A: So what *is* the criterion of sameness here? What do you go by?

B: When it is someone else's images, I go by what he says and does. For example, if he says, "I saw stars both times I was hit," I would say he had the same image both times.[86] But when it is my own image, I apply no criterion, "go by" nothing (sec. 377).

A: Nothing?

B: Here's a ripe cherry. If asked *how* I know it's red, my reply would be, "I've learned English!" (sec. 381). This would actually be a rejection of the "What did you go by?" question.

IMAGINABILITY (SECTIONS 395–397)

A: To be intelligible is to be imaginable; to be imaginable is to be representable in a particular medium.

B: Although a representation sometimes safely points the way to further uses of a sentence, sometimes it obtrudes itself upon us and makes nothing intelligible. (Think of the pictures used by popularizers of modern physics, for example when they explain "the curvature of space." Do they give us any more than the illusion of understanding?)

"THE VISUAL ROOM" (SECTIONS 398–401)

A: When I sit in a room and look around me, I often experience something absolutely my own—something completely subjective and existing outside public space.

B: You are talking, I suggest, about "the visual room," the room with *no* owner. For if you exclude other people from owning it as a matter of logic, then it loses sense to say that *you* own it.

A: I admit I'm not the owner of the visual room in the same sense in which I am owner of the physical room in which we now both sit. I want to say: the owner of the visual room must be the same sort of thing *it* is. (Both are "of the stuff dreams are made on.")

---

86. Cf.: "The mental picture [*Vorstellungsbild*] is the picture which is described when someone describes what he imagines [*seine Vorstellung*]" (sec. 367).

B: Such an "owner" would never be found in his own room, nor outside it either (for "there *is* no outside" [sec. 399]). Some owner!

A: "The visual room" seemed like a discovery!

B: It was—only not of some general feature of perception. Let me suggest that what you were really talking about was the peculiar kind of experience induced by a kind of vacant, "solipsistic" staring. If that's what you were talking about, then I know it well.[87]

"THE FEELING OF AN UNBRIDGEABLE GULF" (SECTIONS 412–414)

A: When, in an introspective mood, I gaze in front of myself at nothing in particular, I want to exclaim in amazement: "And you say THIS, my conscious state, is produced by a process in the brain!"

B: You might make the same exclamation in an entirely different, more mundane context: that of a psychological experiment with you as subject. The experimenter sends an electric current through an area of your brain. Amazed at the experience it stimulates, you exclaim: "And you say *this* is merely the result of the electric current? It's as though I were really seeing something!"

The latter (mundane, experimental) use is related to the earlier (introspective, "philosophical") use as weaving is related to sitting at an empty loom and going through the motions of weaving (sec. 414). "For philosophical problems arise when language *goes on holiday*" (sec. 38), not when it is at work.

When William James spoke of the self as introspectible "motions in the head," he was (as it were) taking the word *self* on a holiday. Introspection had revealed to him, not the meaning of a word in its everyday use, but "the state of a philosopher's attention when he says the word 'self' to himself and tries to analyze its meaning" (sec. 413).

PHILOSOPHICAL ANTHROPOLOGY (SECTION 415)

We have been contributing in these investigations to a kind of anthropology—the kind that offers, not conjectures and curiosities, but reminders of everyday things we normally overlook.

Giving and obeying orders, describing the appearance of an object, expressing one's feelings and impressions, etc.: these (to echo sec. 25) are as much a part of our natural history as walking, eating, playing, etc.

---

87. On "a peculiar kind of experience," see *PI*, p. 209: "It is only if someone . . . is master of such and such, that it makes sense to say he has had *this* experience./ . . . [W]hat we have here is a modified concept of *sensation*" (cf. p. 230 c). On an interesting connection between "solipsistic staring" and schizophrenia, see Louis A. Sass, *The Paradoxes of Delusion*.

(In the course of a seminar on the "hermeneutic circle," the idea that the understanding is already in the presence of that for which it searches, Martin Heidegger asked his students to imagine someone trying to get out of a room: first by a window, which proves too high, finally by the chimney, which proves too narrow; if only he would turn around, he would see that the door has been open all along. I want to connect that image—which Heidegger attributed to Wittgenstein—with his famous pronouncement in *Letter on Humanism*: "Language is the house of being." I want to say: We are not always at home in our own house; what makes us uncomfortable would be evident if only we looked around us in a new way.[88])

CONSCIOUSNESS (SECTIONS 416–427)

We are inclined to think of consciousness as an object of (introspective) experience and to imagine that "I am conscious" records an item of indubitable knowledge. Fighting against this temptation requires focusing on the circumstances in which the sentence "I am conscious" would have a use.

"The chief must be conscious" (sec. 419). When would you say that? Whom would you be informing?

A patient recovering from anaesthesia might whisper, "I'm conscious" to the nurse. He is thereby giving her a signal. He does not say this after "observing his own consciousness" but after observing that the nurse thinks he's still unconscious. He might just as well have said "Hello" (sec. 416).

"Human beings are their own witness that they are conscious": to say this is to confuse a grammatical remark with an empirical observation. (Cf. sec. 281.) He who conceives it as an empirical fact must give an account of what it would be like if human beings were *not* conscious. (Cf. sec. 420.)

Could human beings behave just as they normally do and not be conscious? (sec. 418). How are we to make sense of that? Are they perhaps *pretending* to be conscious?

"Human beings are conscious." We might say this in the course of training foreigners in the use of "human being" (or "conscious"). We would be preparing them in the use the expression "human being," not conveying a piece of information (or misinformation) about human beings.

"He suffered great torments and tossed about restlessly" (sec. 421). Is it logical to predicate "suffered torments" and "tossed about" of one and the same subject?

---

88. The Wittgenstein image Heidegger quotes (*Heraclitus*, p. 17) is described in more detail in "Wittgenstein as a Teacher," Fann, ed., p. 52. (For the Heidegger quote, see *Basic Writings*, p. 193.)

> It seems paradoxical to us that we should make such a medley, mixing physical states and states of consciousness up together in a *single* report. . . . It is quite usual [however]; so why do we find it paradoxical? Because we want to say that the sentence deals with both tangibles and intangibles at once.—But does it worry you if I say: "These three struts give the building its stability"? Are three and stability tangible?—Look at the sentence as an instrument, and at its sense as its employment. (sec. 421; cf. Z, sec. 126)

Objection: We are not averse to saying things such as, "He embraced her joyfully," in everyday life (when we're "speaking with the vulgar"). But we want to make use of an ontologically truer (purer) language when we "speak with the learned" (for instance about research programs in brain science). We want a language that (as it were) cuts reality at the joints. *Reply*: Do you really want to say (even when alone among the learned) that perhaps "He embraced her joyfully" really means, "His body embraced her and his soul was joyful"? *Objection*: That would be to give a crude dualist analysis. Contemporary philosophers of mind would give a sophisticated materialist analysis. *Reply*: My suggestion is to stop "giving analyses of 'vulgar' propositions"—any analyses. I propose that we instead direct our attention to the circumstances in which we would actually say things such as, "He embraced her joyfully," or, "He pretended to embrace her joyfully," etc. We (philosophers) should then reflect on the purposes of such sentences, their roles in language games. *Objection*: But none of that will enable us to solve the mind/body problem. It is that which has driven me and other thinkers to look for the deep meaning of words such as *joy* and *consciousness*, and *body*. *Reply*: I am suggesting that your problem should disappear once you look beyond forms of words to forms of life. "He embraced her joyfully": stop thinking of this sentence as theory laden. Look at it as an instrument whose use is its employment in the everyday practice of language.

Daniel Dennett, a prominent contemporary philosopher of mind, speaks of Wittgenstein's "interminable logotherapy" and counts himself among the numerous post-Wittgensteinian philosophers who want to achieve *results*—including an "adequate theory of consciousness."[89] Now it is true that Wittgenstein is always looking to (as it were) excavate the kind of questions Dennett craves to answer—always looking to uncover their foundations in misunderstandings of the logic of our language. But he too wants results—of a kind: "*complete* clarity. But that simply means that the philosophical problems should *completely* disappear" (*PI*, sec. 133).

---

89. *Darwin's Dangerous Idea*, p. 141.

PICTURES OF THE SOUL (SECTIONS 420–427)

Images of the soul or mind—of an "inner" as opposed to an "outer" life—are embodied in our forms of representation. They are important parts of the "entire mythology stored within our language" (*PO*, p. 133). But how do these images function in our lives? What, if anything, do we actually do with them?

(An entry in CV suggests that we might use one such image to belittle and alienate ourselves from our bodies: "How humiliating to have to appear like an empty tube which is simply inflated by a mind" [p. 11]. I will have more to say about other, quite different uses of the picture in my subsequent discussions of the soul.)

THE AGREEMENT OF THOUGHT AND REALITY (SECTIONS 428–429)

True thoughts correspond to the facts of the world, false ones do not. But even false thoughts mean something—correspond to how the world *might* have been. So there must be a correspondence between thought and the world deeper even than that of true thoughts with the facts.—That Tractarian insight could be expressed more concretely and less pretentiously as follows: When we want to explain to someone what "red" means in the sentence "That is not red," we point to something that *is* red.

THE LIFE OF A SIGN (SECTIONS 430–432)

Something red becomes a sample of red in the use we make of it, just as a ruler measures in the use we make of it. Compare *RPP*-I, sec. 447:

> To the question "What are all the things measured in physics?," we might answer: lengths, times, brightness of light, weights, etc. But we might learn more if we asked, "How is measuring done?" If one does *this*, one is measuring temperature; if *that*, the strength of a current, etc. (paraphrased)

THE MAGIC OF A WISH (SECTIONS 437–441)

A: A wish seems already to know what will satisfy it—even when the thing is not there at all! (sec. 437)

B: The paradox you sense is due to a false comparison. "I can look for him when he is not there, but not hang him when he is not there" (sec. 462).

A: But I know in advance of experience what will satisfy my wish. How is that possible?

B: Saying, "I want an apple," doesn't mean: I believe an apple will quell my feeling of nonsatisfaction (sec. 440). We learn as children a language game of spontaneously expressing wishes in certain circumstances: in this game the question whether I know what I wish before it's fulfilled cannot arise; nor is the event that stops my wishing necessarily equated with the fulfillment of the wish. (Satisfying my wish may not satisfy *me*.)

(Compare Wittgenstein's *Remarks on Frazer's "The Golden Bough"*: "The representation of a wish is, *eo ipso*, the representation of its realization./ But magic brings a wish to representation; it expresses a wish./ . . . An error arises only when magic is interpreted scientifically."[90])

EXPECTATION AND FULFILLMENT (SECTIONS 452–458)

We want to say that if we could somehow *see* an expectation, then we would also see its fulfillment. But the words *seeing an expectation* are just nonsense— unless they mean "overhearing an expression of expectation." If you expect to hear three knocks at the door, then you should be able to express that expecta- tion—by saying, "I expect three knocks at the door," for instance. If I under- stand that, then I know what to call "the fulfillment of your expectation."

"[T]he similarity of expectation to fulfillment is shown by the fact that both are expressed in the same words in language, not by any further proposi- tion" (*WLL*, p. 33). Compare that with *PR*, p. 72 (paraphrased):

> If someone said, "I expect three knocks," and I asked, "How do you know three knocks exist?," that would make no more sense than asking, "How do you know six feet exist,?" after someone had said, "I believe I'm six feet tall."/ What the *Tractatus* called "objects," "simples," were simply what we can speak of *no matter what may be the case*.

The object of an expectation (or the verification of a belief) is shown in the language used to express it, not in any further (scientific or metaphysical) proposition about the existence of objects.

"But it is surely the *mental process* of expectation that points to its fulfill- ment, not a mere expression!" Compare an expression of expectation to a pointer. The pointer comes to point not through some hocus-pocus of the mind, but in the application a living creature makes of it.

"An expectation contains its fulfillment in the same way an order orders its own execution." Here we say no more than: if an order runs "Do so-and-so," then executing it is called "doing so-and-so."

"MY AIM" (SECTION 464)

"My aim is to teach you to pass from a piece of disguised nonsense to some- thing that is patent nonsense." Two sections earlier we were taught to pass from the disguised (Parmenidean) nonsense of "But he must be somewhere if I

---

90. *PO*, p. 125. Cf. Herbert Fingarette, *Confucius: the Secular as Sacred*, passim.

am looking for him" to the patent (comedic) nonsense of "then he must be somewhere if I don't find him and even if he doesn't exist."

INDUCTION (SECTIONS 472–485)

The character of our certainty that the future will resemble the past is especially clear in primitive instances:

> Nothing could induce me to put my hand into a flame—although after all it is *only in the past* that I have burnt myself./ The belief that fire will burn me is of the same kind as the fear that it will burn me./ [H]ere we see the meaning of certainty. (What it amounts to, not just the meaning of the word "certainty.") (secs. 472-474)

The fire I see is the *object* ("target") of my fear; the fact that fire has burned me in the past is the *cause* of my fear.[91]

Should someone ask me why I believe fire will burn me, I would answer: "Because it has burned me in the past." If he continued in a puzzled voice to ask why *that* is a reason, my response (in an equally puzzled voice would be: "That's just the kind of thing we call a reason for such a belief. So what do you mean?"

Objections: (1) Wittgenstein has not effectively shown that skepticism about induction is illegitimate; (2) he attempts to justify induction by means of a question-begging "paradigm case argument."[92]

Replies: (1) His point is that "the skeptical question" so far means nothing—not that it means something illegitimate; (2) when he says, "This is simply what we call a ground" (sec. 480), he is not being defensive about induction; his goal is not "to justify the everyday language game" but to investigate the linguistic source of the skeptic's uneasiness about it. (Perhaps the skeptic is construing "a ground in inductive inference" on the model of "a ground in deduction"—much as Zeno construed "place of a moving arrow" on the model of "place of a stationary arrow"?)[93]

LANGUAGE AND PURPOSE (SECTIONS 491–492)

"I make a plan not merely so as to make myself understood but also in order to get clear about the matter myself" (Z, sec. 329). Therefore, it would be too narrow to define language as a means of communication.

The mercury thermometer was invented for a particular purpose on the basis of laws of nature. "To invent a language" could mean something like

---

91. Sec. 476. Compare *LC*, pp. 13–18.

92. See Harris, "The Problem of Induction in the Late Wittgenstein."

93. See above, p. 2. There is more on induction or "justification by experience" in (for example) *TLP*, 6.31–6.372 and *OC*, secs. 128–135 and 287.

that; or it could mean something more like inventing a new game or dance step.[94]

ORDER-OBEDIENCE/ STIMULUS-RESPONSE (SECTIONS 493–494)

Asked why you applied just *this* color when ordered to paint the wall scarlet, you might give a justification of what you did by (for example) holding up a standard sample of scarlet to the wall for comparison. If your justification fails, you might give the excuse that the lighting was bad when you made the comparison earlier. Asked why you (or anyone) blinks when looking at a strong light, you will answer in terms not of justification and excuse but of "physical causation"—stimulus-response mechanisms, for example.

When we say that the cock calls the hens by crowing, we are comparing the situation with a language game. When we proceed to analyze the crowing into stimulus-response mechanisms, we are dropping the comparison.[95]

> I want to say: It is *primarily* the apparatus of our ordinary language, of our word-language, that we call language; and then other things by analogy or comparability with this. (*PI*, sec. 494)

It is not primarily the crowing of cocks or grunting of musk oxen that we call language. We can call them language by comparison with our language games; but we can also drop the comparison.

Suppose an order of the builder in PI, sec. 2 were analyzed thus: it stimulates the assistant's brain in such a way that it sends out impulses to the muscles of his legs, etc., etc. I think that we would feel the order had lost the character of an order (of language), and that this feeling would make us put the analysis aside. For the activity of order and obedience is a paradigm of what we call a language game: there is nothing by reference to which we call *it* language. Nor does the fact we can compare it with a stimulus-response mechanism give grounds for doubting that paradigmatic status.[96]

(Wittgenstein once compared religious miracles to gesture-language:

> As when a man sits quietly and then makes an impressive gesture, so God lets the world run on smoothly and then accompanies the words of a saint by "a gesture of nature": the trees around him bow, as if in reverence. I don't believe this happened. If I did, that would mean that I was impressed by the occurrence in such a way that I

---

94. On reforming language for particular purposes, see *PI*, sec. 132 and CV, p. 44 a. These passages help us see that the common criticism that Wittgenstein was a hidebound conservative about ordinary language is misconceived.

95. *Orders* are to *stimuli* what *reasons* are to *causes*. But can an order also be a stimulus, and the reason for an action also its cause? See *WLG*, pp. 82–83, and *BB*, p. 13.

96. Compare *PI*, sec. 420, *LFM*, p. 242, and *PO*, pp. 429–444.

couldn't help reacting to it as to a *symbolic* occurrence, not a mere stimulus. [CV, p. 45, paraphrased])

GRAMMATICAL/EMPIRICAL (SECTIONS 495–498)

It is an empirical proposition that people generally follow the sign "<——" by going left. It is a grammatical proposition that going left is the *correct* way to follow the sign.

> Orange is between red and yellow.
> Al hit the ball = The ball was hit by Al.
> Two negatives yield an affirmative; three negatives, a negative again.[97]

These propositions are grammatical: they function to teach rules of our language, or remind us of them. They are to be contrasted with "empirical rules"—for example the rule that warns cooks to remove every speck of yolk from the white when making meringue:

> "[C]ooking" is defined by its end, whereas "speaking" is not. That is why the use of language is in a certain sense autonomous, as cooking and washing are not. You cook badly if you are guided in your cooking by rules other than the right ones; but if you follow other rules than those of chess you are *playing another game*; and if you follow grammatical rules other than such-and-such ones, that does not mean you say something wrong, no, you are speaking of something else. (Z, sec. 320)

It makes no sense to ask whether our grammatical rules are "the correct ones": in *that* sense they are arbitrary.

> If someone says the rules of negation [for example] are not arbitrary because negation could not be such that "Not not p = *not* p," all that could be meant is that the latter rule [equating double negation with emphatic negation] would not correspond to the English word "negation." The objection that the rules are not arbitrary comes from the feeling that they are responsible to the meaning. But how is the meaning of "negation" defined, if not by the rules? "Not not p = p" [the standard double negation rule] does not follow from the meaning of "not" but *constitutes* it. . . . If it is said that the rules . . . are not arbitrary inasmuch as they must not contradict each other, the reply is that if there were a contradiction among them we should [would] simply no longer call certain of them

---

97. In this paragraph I am drawing from the passages printed beneath the line on *PI*, p. 147.

rules. "It is part of the grammar of the word 'rule' that if 'p' is a rule, [then] 'p and not p' is not a rule." (*WLA*, p. 4)[98]

If you say that the double-negation rule *must* have been contained in the original cancelling-a-proposition meaning of negation, you are merely inventing a myth of meaning. ("Of course, we say: 'all this is involved in the concept itself' . . . —but what that means is that we incline to *these* determinations of the concept" [*RFM*, p. 409].)

NONSENSE (SECTIONS 499–500)

What does it mean to say, "This combination of words makes no sense"? *Remarks on the Philosophy of Psychology* provides a helpful example:

> "A contradiction doesn't make sense" does not mean that the sense of a contradiction is nonsense.—We exclude contradictions from language; we have no clear-cut use for them, and we don't want to use them. (*RPP*-II, sec. 290)

Consider the series "red circle, bright circle, large circle . . . ": although we *might* extend it to include "*square* circle," we do not. We exclude the phrase from language not because it "means something impossible" (for it means nothing) but because we have no use for it, and no reason to give it a use.

The quoted passage from *RPP* continues with the example, "It's raining but I don't believe it."[99] Calling it nonsense is a way of objecting to its inclusion in the series to which it superficially belongs, namely:

> It's raining but *you* don't believe it.
> It's raining but *she* doesn't believe it. Etc.

"But under unusual circumstances," the passage continues,

> that sentence could be given a clear sense. [For example:] If there were such a thing as "automatic" speech then we couldn't dispute such an utterance, or try to prove a mistake on the part of the one who speaks it. Thus we would not play the same language games with automatic speech as we do with the usual kind. (*RPP* II, secs. 290–291)

Here I am reminded by what was said in *PI*, sec. 499: "If I surround an area with a fence . . . , the purpose may be to prevent someone from getting in or

---

98. The sentence quoted by Ambrose/Macdonald is from *PG*, p. 304. I have added some emphases to their text, and substituted English for some of their symbols./ For the sense in which the standard double negation rule is *not arbitrary*, see *LFM*, pp. 242–243.

99. This relates to "Moore's paradox," the topic of *PI*-II, x.

out; but it may also be part of a game and the players are supposed, say, to jump over the boundary. . . . "

SENSE, UNDERSTANDING, MEANING (SECTIONS 501–514)

A: "A thought is a proposition [or sentence] with a sense. The totality of propositions is language" (*TLP*, 4–4.001).

B: Although I know that "It's raining" is a proposition with sense, I would not know what to say if asked, "*What* sense?"

A: Think of the sense of the sentence as its content—as *in* it, not as something outside it to which it points. Then reject the suggestion that you ought to be able to say what the sense is.[100]

B: "I have *n* friends and $n^2 + 2n + 2 = 0$." Although this sentence makes sense, it certainly does not *show* its sense. I *calculate* the sense, then put it into words (sec. 513).

A: But that's a special case and should not be taken as a model of everything we call a sentence with sense.

B: A sentence is just signs! How can it "show its sense"?

A: When we ask someone something and she answers with a sign, we don't raise the objection, "But that's a mere answer!" (sec. 503).

B: But how do I know what she means when I have nothing but the signs?

A: That makes as little sense as: "How does *she* know what she means when she has nothing but the signs?" (sec. 504).

B: *She* certainly knows what she means. Suppose she is giving you an order. You will have to understand her before you can obey.

A: Of course. But from that it does not follow that there must be a particular mental state halfway between hearing an order and obeying it. For we do not use the word *understanding* as the name of such a state: to think that we do is to represent our practice of language in undue simplification.[101]

---

100. "The limit of language is shown by its being impossible to describe the fact which corresponds to (is the translation of) a sentence, without simply repeating the sentence" (*CV*, p. 10; cf. *BB*, p. 167).

101. Compare *BB*, pp. 143–144: "There is a kind of general disease of thinking which always looks for (and finds) what would be called a mental state from which all our acts spring as from a reservoir. . . . "

B: A certain experience stands behind my words whenever I *mean* what I say (sec. 507). You're neglecting that.

A: I'm used to the Fahrenheit scale. When I tell you the temperature in Celsius, something seems to be missing—I'm not used to that scale. Is that the sort of thing you mean?

B: I said, "*a b c d*" and meant *The weather is fine*. While I was saying it, I was having the same experiences we normally have when we say, and mean, "The weather is fine." That's what I mean.

A: How do you know you were having precisely those experiences (sec. 509)?

B: Surely *I* know what I meant when I said, "*a b c d*"!

A: You sound like the philosopher who says he meant something by the sentence "I am here" even when he couldn't say how, on what occasions it is used (sec. 514).

PICTURING (SECTIONS 514–524)

A: Is a rose in the dark red, or not red?

B: That question calls up two, alternative pictures: the first of a black expanse; the second of a rose in full color surrounded by black. Choosing the second picture I answer *red*.

A: We do speak of red and white roses in the dark; we do not speak of distinguishing them by sight in the dark: we need to dwell on these linguistic commonplaces—and to reject the original question as nonsense.

B: It makes sense to me!

A: But can't we mistakenly think we understand something and later come to acknowledge the mistake? For example, we might be persuaded by a mathematical demonstration that we cannot really imagine something we believed we could imagine ("the construction of a heptagon," for instance). Such demonstrations "lead us to revise what counts as the domain of the imaginable" (sec. 517).

B: Do you want to say that what is imaginable (logically possible) depends on what our mathematics allows?

A: Yes. And I want to add a point about the nature of mathematics. Mathematics is a grammatical activity: it helps bound the domain of "logically possible," meaningful discourse.

B: Do you want to say that logic and mathematics are *arbitrary?* That's what your comparison with grammar seems to suggest.

A: But grammar is not entirely arbitrary. This shows up in the fact that "it is not every sentence-like formation that we know how to do something with, not every technique that has application in our lives."[102]

VARIETIES OF UNDERSTANDING (SECTIONS 525–533)

Our word *understanding* covers a family of cases. We speak of understanding not only sentences, but also pictures, diagrams, themes in music, people, and cultures. And there is variety within each case as well. For example:

> We speak of understanding a sentence in the sense in which it can be replaced by another which says the same; but also in the sense in which it cannot be replaced by any other. (Any more than one musical theme can be replaced by another.) (sec. 531)

Then shall we say that "understanding" has two different meanings here? No. For we want to apply the word to both, want to say that these diverse uses make up and characterize the *concept* of understanding (sec. 532).

"But in the second case, how can one explain the expression, transmit one's comprehension?" (sec. 533). Ask yourself how one leads anyone to comprehend a poem or a musical theme. The answer to this tells us how meaning is explained here.[103]

ASPECTS (SECTIONS 534–539)

Aspect perception includes: hearing a word in a particular sense (sec. 534), feeling the ending of a scale as an ending (sec. 535), hearing a musical chord "as a modulation first into this, then into that key" (sec. 536), etc.

I see a picture representing a smiling face. What do I do if I take the smile now as kind, now as malicious? I might imagine the smiler smiling down first upon a child at play, then on the suffering of an enemy (sec. 539).

MEANING AND FEELING (SECTIONS 540–546)

A: When longing makes me cry out, "O, if only she would come!" isn't it the *feeling* that gives the words meaning (sec. 544)?

B: If you want to say that the feeling gives the individual words their meaning, then I don't understand. If you want to remind us that a cry can be

---

102. Based on *PI*, sec. 520; cf. sec. 303 and p. 230c. Compare *RFM*, pp. 120 and 401–403 on the sentence-like formations known as "Russell's paradox" and "the liar."

103. On understanding music, see *CV*, pp. 69–70 and *LC*, "Lectures on Aesthetics," passim. On understanding people, see Peter Winch, "Can We Understand Ourselves?" On understanding poetry, see Kenneth Koch, "The Language of Poetry."

full of meaning in the sense that much can be gathered from it, then I understand (sec. 543).

A: Can one say that the feeling gave *truth* to my words (sec. 544)?

B: Yes. And from this you can see how the concepts of meaning and truth merge here (ibid.).

A: When I exclaim, "I *hope* he'll come!," doesn't my feeling give the word its meaning (sec. 545)?

B: Hope is not a certain feeling that gives the word *hope* its meaning—for then the truthfully expressed sentence "I do *not* hope he'll come" would be nonsense (sec. 545).

A: Doesn't feeling give words a special ring?

B: Words may have a special ring when they're pronounced with feeling. Words can be wrung from us like a cry; they can be hard to say, as in a confession of weakness. "Words are also deeds" (sec. 546).[104]

TWO MEANINGS OF "IS" (SECTIONS 558–559)

A: "The rose is red." In that proposition the verb functions quite differently from how it functions in "Twice two is four."

B: As I reflect on that difference, I am led to compare the two propositions to two machines with one interchangeable part—a part that functions very differently in the different mechanisms.

A: But, while in a machine the functioning of the parts may be hidden away in a black box, in a proposition nothing is hidden: the functioning of the words must come to light in our operating with them (sec. 559).[105]

B: What do you mean?

A: When we replace "is" by "equals" in "Twice two is four," we get an equivalent proposition; when we replace it by "equals" in "The rose is red," we get nonsense. This is the sort of thing that brings to light the *essential* difference between the two uses of "is"—the difference in meaning.

104. Compare CV, p. 35 (on the sense in which self-mastery is a prerequisite of truth-telling), and *PI*, pp. 222–223 (on the criteria for a true, i.e., truthful confession).
105. On the "meaning body" alluded to at the end of sec. 559, see *PG*, p. 54.

ESSENTIAL/INESSENTIAL (SECTION 560–570)

We want to call the union of the two uses of "is" under the one word *inessential*. But how do we decide what to call "essential"? Is there something behind a word that shapes its grammar?—"Behind"? Is there something behind the fact that in checkers a king is marked by putting one piece on top of another (sec. 562)? Anyone who understands the point of the game certainly won't think it essential.

A game is defined by its rules, yes. But a game also has a point. We would be puzzled by a rule in a board game requiring players to rotate a piece three times before every move. What's the point, we would wonder—to discourage hasty moves? Compare Philippa Foot:

> Someone who said that clapping the hands three times in an hour was a good action would have first to answer the question "How do you mean?" . . . [W]ithout a special background, there is no possibility of answering the question "What's the point?"[106]

If I understand the character of physics aright—its point, its spirit— then it is possible to "play its language games" in inches as well as centimeters. The difference is inessential—a mere matter of convenience. It would be different if a system of measurement demanded more time and trouble than we could give it (secs. 568–569).

Concepts are instruments: they express, channel, and sometimes transform our interests and investigations.[107]

PSYCHOLOGICAL CONCEPTS (SECTIONS 571–592)

It would be misleading to distinguish psychological from physical concepts by their subject matter. For seeing, expecting, etc. are not the subject of psychology in the same sense the movement of bodies, electrical phenomena, etc. are the subject of physics. The physicist observes falling bodies, tides and other physical phenomena; the psychologist observes the utterances and behavior of the seeing, expecting subject.

"Observing, expecting, etc. are mental states; solidity, hardness, etc., physical states." This is true but not very enlightening. In order to get clear

---

106. From "Moral Beliefs," *Proceedings of the Aristotelian Society*, 1958–1959. Compare Bouwsma, *Conversations*, pp. 5–6 (on Wittgenstein's negative reaction to Malcolm's suggestion that Cesare Borgia might have made "Trample on other men's toes all I can" his ethical principle).

107. See Diamond's "Losing Your Concepts" for an argument against the tendency in analytical philosophy to reduce understanding concepts to knowing how to group things under them.

about these concepts, we need to recall what, in particular cases, we regard as criteria for their application.

"He was expecting her." This might mean no more than "He would have been surprised if she hadn't come." But it might mean "Her coming occupied his thoughts." If his behavior gives us no reason to doubt his sincerity, then we will take what he tells us as the criterion for how (if at all) he was expecting her (sec. 577).[108]

Belief, like expectation, may or may not involve thinking (sec. 574). I may believe a chair will bear me without having any thoughts about it. But: "In spite of all he did, I retained the belief . . . "; *here* there is thought (sec. 575). "Belief" and "thought" are different conceptual pathways that at times intersect.

A belief is a state—a state of the individual said to have it. And it is only of living human beings and animals that behave like them that we can say: they believe such-and-such.[109] "We might say that the dog believes he will be beaten, but not that he will be beaten tomorrow" (adapted from *PI*, sec. 650).

I am sitting in my room believing (or hoping or fearing) that So-and-so will come. Suppose now that an instant of my mental state could be isolated, cut out of context. Would it still be belief (hope, fear)? Would a smiling face still *smile* if isolated from the human face (sec. 583)?

PHILOSOPHICAL TEMPTATIONS (SECTIONS 593–609)

There are temptations to be resisted if we are to think clearly about the concepts that interest us as philosophers. We are tempted:

- to nourish our thinking with only one type of example

  > I stop short, look at the object or man questioningly or mistrustfully, [and] say "I find it all strange."—But the existence of this feeling of strangeness does not give us a reason for saying that every object which we know well . . . gives us a feeling of familiarity. (sec. 596)

- to impose requirements of the form "But it *must* be like that"

  > We think that, as it were, the place once filled by the feeling of strangeness must surely be occupied *somehow*. (ibid)

---

108. This section concludes with the remark that a language in which different verbs were consistently used in these cases might be more suitable than our own for understanding psychology. This should be relevant to the current discussion of "folk psychology"and its limitations.

109. Adapted from PI, sec. 281. Cf.: "The living human being is as essential to our concepts of the mental as the chessboard is to chess" (Malcolm, *Problems*, p. 30).

- to hypostatize feelings and processes

> Just as a German may speak English as if he were translating
> "unconsciously" from the German, so we often think as if in our
> thinking we were translating a more primitive mode of thought
> into ours. (sec. 597, paraphrased; cf. *PI*, sec. 32)

- to entertain inappropriate paradigms

> It is easy to have a false picture of the processes called "recogniz-
> ing"; as if recognizing always consisted in comparing two impres-
> sions with one another. (sec. 604)

INDESCRIBABILITY (SECTION 610)

"'Essentially inexpressible' means that it makes no sense to talk of a more complete expression" (*PG*, p. 45). To say that something makes no sense is "to
exclude a certain combination of words from the sphere of language " (*PI*, sec.
499). For example, it is to exclude combinations of words that purport to give
a matter-of-fact description of a certain aroma or musical theme. Compare:
"The *tao* that can be spoken is not the true *tao*."[110] And compare the following
from Wittgenstein's "Lecture on Ethics":

> When it's urged against me that what we *mean* in attributing
> absolute value to an experience is just a fact like other facts, then I
> at once see clearly that I would reject every significant description
> that anyone could possibly suggest . . . (*PO*, p. 44, paraphrased)

When he speaks of inexpressibility, Wittgenstein is never making an episte-
mological point—for example, an intuitionist (or gnostic) claim that some
people have knowledge of things that by their very nature cannot be put into
words. His point is always grammatical: he is either excluding, or remarking
on the exclusion of, some combination of words from the sphere of speech.
When, in this section, he called coffee aroma indescribable, he was making a
remark as a speaker of ordinary language; when, in his ethics lecture, he called
absolute value indescribable, he was speaking for himself: "Here . . . all I can
do is to step forth as an individual and speak in the first person."[111]

Whenever I want to fix my mind on what I mean by absolute value, I
think of an experience I want to describe as "the state of mind in which one is

---

110. *Tao Te Ching*, first line. Cf. Novalis: "Looking everywhere for the unconditioned
[*das Unbedingte*], we always find only things [*Dinge*]" (Fieguth, *Deutsche Aphorismen*, p.
78, my translation).

111. *WVC*, p. 117, commenting on his ethics lecture. The ethics lecture (where the
absolute/relative value distinction is introduced) is reprinted in *PO*. Cf. p. 25, above.

inclined to say 'I am safe, nothing can injure me whatever happens'" (PO, p. 41). But "to be safe essentially means that it is physically impossible that certain things should happen to me, and therefore it is nonsense to say that I am safe *whatever* happens" (PO, p. 42):

> So now I see that my "description" of absolute value was nonsensical, not because I hadn't found the right expression for it, but that its nonsensicality was its very essence. For all I wanted to do with it was just to *go beyond* the world, that is to say beyond significant language. (PO, p. 42, paraphrased)

It is of course important in everyday life to distinguish safe from unsafe situations, and to avoid the latter as far as possible. When I speak of "an experience of *absolute* safety," I am intentionally going beyond the significant, everyday use of the word "safety." I want to express a certain attitude toward the pursuit of safety: one that takes it seriously, but only up to a point—one that I connect with Dante's words, "In His will is our peace." ("And saying so to some/ Means nothing; others it leaves/ Nothing to be said."[112])

VOLUNTARY/INVOLUNTARY (SECTIONS 611–630)

"When I raise my arm, it goes up." The philosophical problem arises when we seek to specify "what's left over" when I subtract the fact that my arm goes up from the fact that I raise it. Wittgenstein's advice is: stop insisting there must be something left over (inner or outer) that the volition consists in; start recalling and describing the circumstances in which we speak of the voluntary and involuntary. Recall, for instance, that "voluntary movement is marked by the absence of surprise" (sec. 628), so that someone surprised that her own arm is going up will not regard the movement as voluntary.[113]

Responding to the objection that the word *joy* must surely designate something (if not a behavior, then a feeling), Wittgenstein remarks that it designates nothing at all: "Neither any inward nor any outward thing" (Z, sec. 487). As with "voluntary" and so many other words of philosophical interest, we feel here the strong pull of the object-designation model of language. We will have to break away from it if we are to be freed from the obsessive inner/outer dialectic of modern philosophy.

---

112. From "Nothing to Be Said," by Philip Larkin; quoted in Richter, p. 243. For more on these matters, see the essays headed "God," below.
113. "How do you know that you have raised your arm?" (sec. 625). Does this question have an obvious answer ("because I felt it"), or is it really nonsense? (The upcoming section, "Kinaesthesia" is relevant here.)

"PRIVATE MAPS" (SECTIONS 653–655)

Philosophical questions call for *noting* language games. When we seek to go beyond that by "grounding the language game in some experience," we end up, at most, with the illusion of an explanation.

"Could I now say, 'I read off my having then meant to do such and such as if from a map, although there is no map'?" (sec. 653). The following case sheds light on that question:

> I tell someone I walked a certain route using a map I prepared beforehand. I show him my "map," which consists of lines on a piece of paper; but I am unable to explain how these lines are the map of my movements. Yet I did follow the drawing with the characteristic behavior of someone following a map. (sec. 653, paraphrased)

We might be inclined to call my scribbles "a private map." That would be understandable and unobjectionable. But we would be deluding ourselves if we thought we had thereby *explained* why I went the way I did.

"What then does one go by in reporting ones's past wishes and intentions?" Why think there must be something (perhaps a memory image) from which you read off your intentions and wishes?

(Compare *CV*, p. 17: "Philosophers often behave like little children who scribble some marks on a piece of paper at random then ask the grown-up 'What's that?'—It happened like this: the grown-up had drawn pictures for the child several times and said: 'this is a man,' 'this is a house,' etc. And then the child makes some marks too and asks: what's *this* then?")

VARIETIES OF TELLING, REMEMBERING, INTENDING (SECTIONS 656–693)

I tell someone what I did and also what my intention was. In the latter case, I am also telling something about myself—but not on the grounds of self-observation.

Compare "I was then going to say" with "I could then have gone on." In the first case, I was remembering an intention; in the second case, I was remembering having understood something.

Is "remembering having meant something" remembering a process? If so, then it should make sense to ask when it began and what course it took (its beginning, middle, and end).

Compare the surface grammar of the verb *to mean* (the form of the words) with its depth grammar (its actual function in the language game). For example: "Imagine someone pointing to his cheek with an expression of pain and saying, 'abracadabra.' . . . By 'abracadabra' [he continues] I mean toothache" (sec. 665). He has given us his definition of that strange sound, not (as the visible form of his words suggest) the description of what went on in him when he uttered it. Another example: "You're in pain and simultaneously hear a piano nearby being tuned. You say, 'It'll soon stop'; then you explain, 'I meant the *pain*'" (sec. 666, modified).[114] The surface grammar of your explanation (its likeness to "I kicked the ball," for example) suggests that "meaning something" consists in somehow "doing something to something" (concentrating one's attention on it, for example). The speciousness of the suggestion dawns on us once we consider the case of someone saying, "It'll soon get better!," while he simulates pain. We can say he means the pain even though he *has* no pain to be concentrating on (sec. 667).

Kinaesthesia
(Part II, Section viii)

William James compared kinaesthesia (sensation of the movement and position of one's limbs) with sense perception (seeing, touching, etc.)[115] I try to convey Wittgenstein's investigation of James's comparison in the following dialogue:

A: I know your fingers are moving and your legs crossed by looking at them; I know my fingers are moving and my legs crossed without looking.

B: Suppose a hospital patient tells the nurse that his legs are crossed. If pulling back the covers reveals that they're not, then he didn't know, after all. Either he was lying, or . . .

A: The point is that *normally* we know the position of our own limbs without looking at them.

B: What do you mean? How are you using "know"?

A: In this context, "knowing the position without looking" only means "being able to describe it accurately without looking."

B: What enables us to do that? Don't we go by certain feelings in our muscles and joints?

A: Suppose I inform a blind man that my legs are crossed, and he responds with a skeptical "How do you know?" That might make sense if he thinks I'm under local anaesthesia. Normally, however, it would not make sense. For, although my knowledge of the position of my limbs always has cer-

---

114. Norman Malcolm has a most illuminating discussion of this and related sections in "Wittgenstein and the Nature of Mind," chapter 6 of his *Thought and Knowledge*.

115. For more on kinaesthesia in general and the reference to William James in particular, see Hallett's *Companion*, pp. 640 ff. *BB*, p. 51, and *LPP*, pp. 310–313 are also relevant.

tain causal conditions (perhaps including "not being under anesthesia"), normally it does not have epistemic grounds. Perhaps this analogy will help:

> I may be able to tell the direction from which a sound comes only because it affects one ear more strongly than the other, but I don't feel this in my ears; yet it has its effect: I *know* the direction from which the sound comes; for instance, I look in that direction. (p. 185 c)

Although the particular effect of the sound on my ears may cause me to look in a certain direction, that particular effect is not my *reason* for looking in that direction. I had no reason. There was no "how I knew the direction."

B: I feel kinaesthetic sensations in my legs, as I do not feel the subtle difference in the way the sound affects one ear more than another. So your analogy is weak.

A: Imagine this:

> I let my index finger make an easy pendulum movement of small amplitude. I either hardly feel it, or don't feel it at all . . . [and yet] I can describe the movement exactly. (p. 185 b)

You speak of sensations advising us of the movement and position of our limbs. I can make no sense of such talk unless I imagine an unusual, special context:

> For example, if you do not know, as a normal person does, whether your arm is stretched out, you might find out by a piercing pain in the elbow. (p. 185 e)

In the normal case you don't find out about the movement or position of your limbs by attending to sensations—or to anything else. (Suppose you move your index finger and the pain is so great that all other sensations in the same place are submerged. Would that make you unable to describe its movement without looking?)[116]

Aspect Perception
(Part II, Section xi)

The bulk of this longest section of *PI* is on aspect perception (pp. 193–214). The remainder concerns: experiencing the meaning of a word (pp. 214–216); meaning, intending, thinking (pp. 217–218); the "physiognomy" of words

---

116. If we insist that knowledge of the movement of our limbs must always have grounds ("if only unconscious grounds"), then we are expressing dissatisfaction with the grammar of everyday language. And then we need to look for what's behind the dissatisfaction. On this see Paul Johnston, *Wittgenstein and Moral Philosophy*, pp. 40–45.

(pp. 218–219); internal speech (p. 220); knowledge, certainty, agreement (pp. 221–229). The analysis to follow is on aspect perception and experiencing the meaning of a word.[117]

SEEING AND SEEING-AS

As with many of our concepts, the concept of seeing has a complexity we tend to underestimate. The complexity begins to emerge once we distinguish two sorts of answer to the question "What do you see?":

1. "Now I see their faces" (while before their backs were turned);
2. "Now I see the likeness between their faces."

Perhaps I saw the two faces in the past without noticing their likeness; when I do notice it, I may have a visual experience comparable to the "dawning of a new aspect" experienced with certain drawings, pictures, and patterns. For example, first I saw the schematic cube with the *a*'s in front, now with the *b*'s:

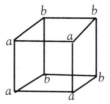

What changes when I see the schematic cube first one way, then another? Not the picture itself but the *aspect* under which it is seen. But what is that? What do I see when I see an aspect?—The last two questions make it sound as if there *must* be a better answer to the question "What changes?" than simply "the aspect." They are questions in search of a theory.

The theory that suggests itself is that what changes is a certain "private object"—an *inner picture*:

> "After all my visual impression isn't the *drawing*; it is this—which I can't show to anyone."—Of course it is not the drawing, but neither is it anything of the same category, which I carry within myself./ The concept of the "inner picture" is misleading, for this concept uses the "*outer* picture" as a model; and yet the uses of the words for these concepts are no more like one another than the uses of "numeral" and "number." (And if one chose to call numbers 'ideal numerals,' one might produce a similar confusion.) (PI, p. 196)

---

117. *PI*-II, sec. xi is drawn from the much larger body of remarks on seing-as contained in *RPP*. Paul Johnston's *Rethinking the Inner* and Stephen Mulhall's *Being in the World* are helpful secondary sources. (I am indebted to them both.)

To use a phrase made famous by Gilbert Ryle: the "inner picture theory" makes a *category mistake* in the way it lumps together the drawing itself with the different ways of seeing it.[118] What belong to different logical categories (the figure and its aspects) are represented as if they were two species of the same genus ("pictures: outer and inner").[119]

Aspect perception covers a variety of cases. Compare "seeing the aspects of the double cross" with "seeing the aspects of Jastrow's duck-rabbit," for example:

> You only "see the duck and rabbit aspects" if you are already conversant with the shapes of those two animals. There is no analogous condition for seeing the aspects [of the double cross—white cross on black ground, black cross on white ground]. (*PI*, p. 207 i)

Note also that some cases of aspect perception require imagination in a way others do not. For example, the triangle

can be seen as

> a wedge, as an arrow or pointer, as an overturned object . . . , and as various other things. (*PI*, p. 200 c)/ It is possible to take the duck-rabbit simply for the picture of a rabbit, the double cross simply for the picture of a black cross, but not to take the bare triangular figure for the picture of an object that has fallen over. To see this aspect of the triangle demands *imagination*. (p. 207 j)/ [Also,] doesn't it take imagination to hear something as a variation on a particular theme? (p. 213 d)

---

118. On "category mistake," see the first chapter of Ryle's *Concept of Mind* (where we find the memorable example of the visitor to Oxford who wanted to see the university but was disappointed at being shown only the colleges). Cf. *RPP*.I, secs. 534–536.

119. Readers of the *Tractatus* may want to connect *PI* on pictures and their aspects with *TLP*, 2.172: "A picture cannot . . . depict its pictorial form: it displays it." Cf. 2.172–2.18 and 4.121–4.1212.

When we see—or hear—something as something, we are indeed *perceiving* something in so seeing or hearing it. And yet the concept "I am now seeing it as ___" is akin to "I am now imagining such-and-such" (the Taj Mahal, for example). For like imagination and unlike "plain seeing," seeing-as is subject to the will. Thus: "There is such an order as 'Imagine *this*,' and also: 'Now see the figure like *this*'; but not: 'Now see this leaf green'" (p. 213 f). (Perceiving the color of a leaf would be squarely on the "seeing" side of the seeing/seeing-as dichotomy.[120])

Imaginative aspect perception appears to be of considerable service in aesthetic and mathematical thinking:

> [I]n conversation on aesthetic matters we use the words: "You have to see it like *this*, this is how it is meant." (*PI*, p. 202 k)/ [W]hen one discovers . . . that two right isosceles triangles put together give a rectangle [,one says:] "Oh, that has never struck me; but now I see it must be so." We do not say this in the case of a genuine experiment. (*WLA* , p. 179–180)

We present the outcome of an experiment in a table or diagram; we represent it as one among a range of other outcomes. While the results of (honest) experimental research may be called a discovery but not invention, the results of mathematical research may (I suggest) be called either discovery or invention—just as seeing-as may be called seeing or insight (or both).

Seeing-as in mathematical research is in the service of concept formation:

> Suppose we visually divide | | | | into two groups of two. . . . Seeing the strokes in pairs *suggests* a rule, 2 + 2 = 4. A certain symbolism readily goes with a certain aspect which strikes us when we look at a thing. (*WLA*, p. 180)

To make "2 + 2 = 4" a rule is to assign it a special role in the language game of counting and measuring, to (as it were) place it in the vault of the Bureau of Weights and Measures, along with the standard meter bar.[121] There are nor-

---

120. *Objection:* Noticing a color is never *plain* seeing because it always involves culture-relative concepts. *Reply:* Your premise is not relevant to our everyday distinction between seeing and seeing-as. *Objection:* I want to say that *all* seeing is seeing-as. *Reply:* Then you would be using the word "in a typically metaphysical way" (*BB*, p. 46). But to what point?

121. See *PI*, sec. 50, and the following from *RFM*, p. 237: "The limit of the empirical—is *concept-formation.*/ What is the transition I make from 'It will be like this' to 'It *must* be like this'? I form a different concept. One involving something that was not there before. When I say: 'If these derivations are the same then it *must* be that . . . ,' I

mally reasons for the rules we adopt—and here we might cite aspects that strike us when we look at things. But the rules are never to be *equated with* the reasons. (To do that would be to give a "psychologistic" or other reductive account of mathematics.)

INTERNAL RELATIONS

"The color of the visual impression corresponds to the color of the object (this blotting paper looks pink to me, and is pink)—the shape of the visual impression to the shape of the object (it looks rectangular to me, and is rectangular)—but what I perceive in the dawning of an aspect is not a property of the object, but an internal relation between it and other objects" (p. 212a). Suppose we're looking at a set of hoops. I say: "Some look elliptical, some round." You say: "Some *are* elliptical, some round; you have correctly perceived the shapes of the hoops." I add: "I see the likeness between ellipses and circles: ellipses are elongated circles." When I saw the elliptical shape of the hoop, I saw a property of the object; when I saw the ellipses as elongated circles, I saw a likeness; when I saw the likeness, I perceived an internal relation. You ask: "internal" as opposed to what? Answer: As opposed to "external," i.e., empirical, factual, genetic, historical, temporal. The hoop-maker might have started with circular hoops and transformed some of them into ellipses. The elliptical hoops would be externally related to the round ones he began with. In saying, "The ellipse came from a circle," one *could* be making this empirical statement about the origin of the ellipse. But one could also be expressing the dawning of an aspect, the perception of a new *way* of seeing the ellipse—a perception that might suggest (*has* suggested) a new concept formation. So the same sentence might express first an external relation, a relation between objects (hoops), then an internal relation, a relation between concepts (circle and ellipse).[122]

ASPECT AND MEANING BLINDNESS

Wittgenstein's imagined aspect blind person would agree that what we call "the picture of a balloon" could be used to *symbolize* a balloon. But she would not see and react to it as a balloon. What aspect blindness is to pictures, meaning blindness is to words. For the meaning blind, words have meaning only as

---

am making something into a criterion of identity. So I am recasting my concept of identity."

122. As we can experience "MARCH" first as a month of the year then as a parade command, so we can experience "The ellipse came from the circle" first as an empirical, then as a conceptual remark. Progress in philosophical investigation seems often connected with some such aspect switch.

part of an agreed symbolism; for the rest of us, they have a value of their own and seem to "embody" their meanings.[123]

Sneers and smiles look as different to us as ducks and rabbits. The rare individual to whom the human smile meant nothing might see the sometimes minute facial changes involved in the transition from a smile to a sneer but fail to understand why we now say the face *looks* completely different. Although he might develop empirical rules for interpreting expressions, he would lack real insight and sensitivity. He would be blind to the aspects of that most important of pictures—"the picture of the soul," the human face.[124]

A person's utterances are the primary criterion for thinking he is seeing an aspect—and these may sound nonsensical. I imagine "the aspect blind person" would be totally bewildered at the sight of us pointing at a Jastrow figure and exclaiming, "Now we see a duck, now a rabbit." For while she learned to use the word *see* with the rest of us, she never went on to extend its application to "seeing aspects."

"Blindness" is a privative term, signifying a lack. Shall we speak of "aspect blindness" as a kind of arrested development?

"SEEING THE WORLD ARIGHT" (TLP, 6.54)

Would people blind to the changing aspects of pictures, words, and faces lack anything important? I think they would certainly lack what it takes to be (for example) artists, critics, men of letters, mathematicians, and psychotherapists: the happiness (and unhappiness) proper to these human activities would be closed to them. And here I pose a question: Doesn't a person have to rely on something like aspect perception in order to be—not happy or unhappy *at this or that* but—happy or unhappy *simpliciter*? This question leads us back to "Uncle Ludwig's book on ethics,"[125] the *Tractatus Logico-Philosophicus*.

People who are happy *simpliciter* are people whose "world" is different from that of the unhappy.[126] If the unhappy are to become happy, their world—their life taken as a whole—will have to become altogether different, "as if by accession . . . of meaning" (*NB*, p. 73).

It would be natural to speak of "a certain blindness" in the case of people unable to experience life as either having meaning or lacking it. They would be like the trapper in Jack London's "To Build a Fire":

---

123. See *PI*, p. 218 k on "the familiar physiognomy of a word."

124. See *Z*, sec. 225 ("We *see* emotion . . . ") and Brenner, *Logic and Philosophy*, pp. 124 ff.

125. Although I have unfortunately lost the "Uncle Ludwig" reference, the surprising characterization of the *Tractatus* as a book on ethics is confirmed in Wittgenstein's letter to Ludwig Ficker, reprinted in Englemann, pp. 143–144.

126. Compare *TLP*, 6.43.

> But all this—the mysterious, far-reaching hairline trail, the absence of sun from the sky, the tremendous cold, and the strangeness and weirdness of it all—made no impression on the man. It was not because he was long used to it. . . . The trouble with him was that he was without imagination. He was quick and alert in the things of life, but only in the things, and not in their significances. . . . [127]

Imagination, as we saw, is required for seeing the aspects of some figures and diagrams. But I take it that the really serious and important service of imagination is ethico-religious. In words from Coleridge, here imagination functions to

> disimprison the soul of fact . . . by awakening the mind's attention from lethargy and custom, and directing it to the loveliness and the wonders of the world before us; an inexhaustible treasure, but for which, in consequence of the film of familiarity and selfish solicitude, we have eyes, yet see not . . . [128]

Coleridge distinguished imagination from fancy. If imagination "sees into the life of things," fancy "spreads itself over matters of fact." If imagination is philosophic, fancy is self-assertive.[129] Perhaps it is in the exercise of this "philosophic imagination" that we see the oneness of ethics and aesthetics asserted in *Tractatus* 6.421.

Drawing on Simone Weil, I would develop what I find hinted at in Wittgenstein along the following lines: The ethico-religious challenge is to renounce our human tendency to fancy ourselves the center of the universe; if we meet the challenge, then the transformation we experience will be like the dawning of a new aspect:

> We see the same colors, hear the same sounds, but not in the same way. To empty ourselves of our false divinity is to discern that all points in the world are equally centers.[130]

Concept Formation
(Part II, Section xii)

This brief but important section needs to be supplemented. I begin with a set of quotations.

---

127. With thanks to Cora Diamond.

128. Quoted from *Biographia Literaria* in Willey, *Nineteenth Century Studies*, pp. 21–22.

129. "Sees into the life of things" comes from Wordsworth; "spreads itself over matters of fact," from Hume. The philosophic/self-assertive dichotomy is from Plato's *Phaedo*. Compare J. R. Jones, "Love as Perception of Meaning."

130. *Waiting for God*, p. 159. Cf.: Wittgenstein, *NB*, p. 83; Edelman, "Beauty," p. 9; and Brenner, "Chesterton," p. 318, fn. 19.

NATURE AND CONVENTION

> Roughly speaking, the relation of the grammar of expressions to
> the facts which they are used to describe is that between the meth-
> ods & units of measurement and the results of using these methods
> & units. Now I could describe the shape and size of this room by
> giving its length, breath and height in feet and, just as well by giv-
> ing them in meters. I could also give them in microns. In a way
> therefore you might say that the choice of the units is arbitrary.
> But in a most important sense it is not. There is a most important
> reason why we don't measure the dimensions of a room in microns,
> a reason lying both in the room's size and irregularity of shape, and
> in the use we make of it. So, it is not only the *results* but also the
> *method* that tells us something about the world in which the mea-
> surement takes place. And in this very way the technique of use of
> a word gives us an idea of *very* general truths about the world in
> which it is used, of truths in fact which are so general that they
> don't strike people . . . (*PO*, pp. 448–449)[131]

T.S. Champlin gives these further examples of "such facts as mostly do not
strike us because of their generality" (*PI*, sec. xii a):

> The applicability of the phrase "in the head" to . . . thoughts . . .
> depends on certain very general facts of nature such as that the
> mouth is in the head and that when we speak our words come out of
> our mouths./ A thought "enters our head" because we see and hear
> things with our eyes and ears and they are in our head. . . . You can
> often tell what someone is silently thinking by looking at the expres-
> sion on his face; and the face is where his head is./ ([A] thought in
> one's elbow . . . is not just contingently impossible . . .)[132]

Following Wittgenstein's suggestion that a concept might be compared with a
style of painting, "the Egyptian for instance" (sec. xii c), Champlin, at the
conclusion of his article, invites us to compare the concept of thoughts in the
head with the cartoonist's device of showing unspoken thought in a "bubble"
coming out of a character's head.

"THE REAL FOUNDATIONS" (PI, SECTION 129)

If we want to speak (as well as to think) with the learned, shouldn't we stop
saying things like "The sun rises, the sun sets"? *No*—no more than we should
stop talking about "thoughts in the head." For our everyday language gives us

131. From "Notes for the 'Philosophical Lecture,'" with some sentences modified for
greater intelligibility. (Compare: *TLP*, 6.342; *Z*, secs. 357–358, 364–365; and "Color
Grammar," below.)
132. "Head Colds and Thoughts in the Head," *Philosophy* 68 (1989), pp. 39–48.

concepts, not theories (Z, sec. 223). Nor have modern scientific discoveries dislodged the "very general facts of nature" that surround our everyday concepts and hold them fast. For these are what is most important for us. Philosophical investigation uncovers these familiar but striking aspects of things when it looks into the workings of our language without preconceptions.[133]

AGREEMENT IN LANGUAGE

> If we teach a human being such-and-such a technique by means of examples—that he then proceeds like *this* and not like *that* in a particular new case, or that in this case he gets stuck, and thus that this and not that is the "natural" continuation for him: this of itself is an extremely important fact of nature. (Z, sec. 355)/ For instance: you say to someone "This is red" (pointing); then you tell him "Fetch me a red book"—and he will behave in a particular way. This is an immensely important fact about us human beings. (*LFM*, p. 182)

> "If humans were not in general agreed about the colors of things, if undetermined cases were not exceptional, then our concept of color could not exist." No:—our concept *would* not exist. (Z, sec. 351)

Why "would not" instead of "could not"? "Could not" mis-characterizes our concept, by suggesting that the agreement in question is one of its defining properties. Although the language game of color predication would not exist unless speakers generally agreed in their color predications, the fact of this general agreement does not enter into the meaning of the color words: "The color of an object" does not *mean* "what people generally agree in calling its color." Similarly, although there would be no game of chess unless players generally agreed over when the rules of the game are being obeyed or disobeyed, the fact of this general agreement does not enter into the description of the rules.

Although it is not our agreement that determines the truth of what we say when we describe (for example) the color of a spot, still what we call "describing the color of a spot" is partly determined by a certain agreement in our judgments of color. Similarly:

> It is one thing to describe methods of measurement, and another to obtain and state results of measurement. But what we call "measuring" is partly determined by a certain constancy in the results of measurement. (*PI*, sec. 242)

---

133. Cf. *PI*, secs. 109 and 66.

Thus:

> The procedure of putting a lump of cheese on a balance and fixing
> the price by the turn of the scale would lose its point if it frequently
> happened for such lumps to suddenly grow or shrink for no obvious
> reason. (*PI*, sec. 142)

Similarly: the procedure of describing the appearance of spots in terms of color
would lose its point (its importance in our lives) if such objects suddenly
changed their appearance for no obvious reason.

It is one thing to differ from others on the weight or the color of something, quite another to differ from them in the *procedure* for judging its weight
or its color. The first is a difference in opinion, the second in "language or
form of life" (*PI*, sec. 241). If I say the cheese is one pound and you say that it
isn't, one of us is mistaken. But if people in our society weigh cheese on a balance while those in another ("more primitive") society simply "heft" it, it does
not follow that one is mistaken. Suppose they say it weighs a pound while we
say it weighs a bit less: that would suggest that our concepts are slightly different—we might call their "pound" a rougher, simpler version of ours. Suppose
they say it weighs a pound—except on Fridays: here there would be an even
greater difference in concepts (in language)—but not, again, a mistake ("For a
blunder, that's too big" [*LC*, p. 62]). Suppose, finally, that they frequently disagree among themselves over the weight of the cheese and often come to
blows over it: there would be hardly enough regularity in their "procedure" for
us to call it a method of weighing things. Although "methods of determining
weight" cover, for us, a whole "family" of procedures, *here* (I think) we have
reached a boundary of the concept.[134] We would not want to call what these
people are doing *any* kind of measuring—except perhaps as a joke.[135]

"A CONFUSION PERVADING ALL PHILOSOPHY"

> The fallacy we want to avoid is this: when we reject some form of
> symbolism, we are inclined to look at it as though we had rejected
> a proposition as false. It is wrong to treat the rejection of a unit of
> measure as though it were [like the] rejection of the proposition
> "The chair is three feet high rather than two." This confusion per-
> vades all of philosophy. (*WLA*, p. 69)

---

134. Compare *PI*, p. 225 on "determining length."

135. This section bears on "relativism" and related philosophical theories. While *individual relativists* (like the"diarist" of *PI*, sec. 258) overlook the "agreement in language
and form of life" required for the formation and maintenance of the rule-governed
practice called a "language game," *societal relativists* (and some of their "realist" oppo-
nents) confuse it with the agreement (or disagreement) in opinion that exists only
within a language game.

The belief that "certain concepts are absolutely the correct ones"(*PI*, sec. xii b) would be a manifestation of this confusion. And the remedy for it would be to "imagine certain very general facts of nature different from what we are used to" (ibid). Imagining them otherwise than the way they are, we can "no longer imagine the application of certain concepts" (*Z*, sec. 350). We saw this already in connection with color and weight; the following quotations contain two additional illustrations:

> Imagine, e.g., that all human bodies which exist looked alike, that on the other hand, different sets of characteristics seemed, as it were, to change their habitation among these bodies. Such a set of characteristics might be, say, mildness together with a high pitched voice and slow movements, or a choleric temperament, a deep voice, and jerky movements, and such like. Under such circumstances, although it would be possible to give the bodies names, we should perhaps be as little inclined to do so as we are to give names to the chairs of our dining room set. On the other hand, it might be useful to give names to the sets of characteristics, and the use of these names would now *roughly* correspond to the personal names in our present language. (*BB*, pp. 61–62)

> If human beings could really observe the functioning of others' nervous systems . . . and regulated their dealings with them accordingly, I believe they would not have our concept of pain (e.g.) . . . Their life *would simply look entirely different from ours.* (*LW*-II, p. 40, translation modified)

> We could say people's concepts show what matters to them and what doesn't. But it's not as if this *explained* the particular concepts they have. It is only to rule out the view that we have the right concepts and other people the wrong ones. (There is a continuum between an error in calculation and a different mode of calculating.) (*RC*-III, sec. 293; cf. *PI*, secs. 142–143)[136]

A CONCEPTUALIZED REALITY?

A: Do we always and inescapably perceive a conceptualized reality?

B: *What* reality? Let's look at particular cases. What we see first as a duck then as a rabbit is the Jastrow figure: there's the reality we see (the figure), and its aspects (what we see it as).[137]

---

136. On conceptual change and the possibilities of impoverishment or liberation it may involve, see "Losing Your Concepts," by Cora Diamond.

137. If we call this "conceptualizing," we should beware of confusing it with *interpreting.* For while interpreting is an act, seeing-as (like seeing) is a state. "When we interpret we form hypotheses, which may prove false.—'I am seeing this figure as a . . .' can

A: Isn't reality conceptualized when we look at the pond and exclaim, "It's full of ducks!"?

B: What are you getting at? Are you alluding to the fact that we can't describe what we see without concepts? If so, then the point is, not to say something about human limitations, but to rule out a certain form of words, exclude it from language. Should someone insist that he for one is able to describe to himself (in his own private language?) what he sees without using any concepts, we should say that he is running up against—not limits of human ability—but limits of language.

A: Don't our concepts stand between us and the reality we perceive and describe?[138]

B: Such a question compares concepts to a barrier. Why not compare them to tools?

A: Then are the "tools" right for the job?

B: What job? Aren't there many things we do with concepts?

A: Isn't there a *main* job—describing reality?

B: Look at all that can be meant by "description of reality":

> There is not *one genuine* proper case of such description—the rest being just vague, something which awaits clarification, or which must just be swept aside as rubbish. (*PI*, p. 200; cf. *CV*, p. 60h)

Sometimes we describe what we see "impressionistically," in terms of shapes and colors, lights and shadows; at other times (and usually) we describe it "objectively," in terms of particular objects (churches, haystacks, etc.). Why give any type of concept—any of the ways in which we represent our experience—a transcendent, metaphysical emphasis?

> Think of the recognition of *facial expressions*. Or of the description of facial expressions—which does not consist in giving the measurements of the face! (*PI*, sec. 285)

be verified as little as (or in the same sense as) 'I am seeing bright red'" (*PI*, p. 212e; cf. sec. 201).

138. It appears that some metaphysicians reject the grammatical truism "We must use concepts to describe the objects we see" as if they were rejecting a false factual claim, others (representational realists) distort it by inferring that our concepts must "stand-between" us and the objects they represent. Idealists reject the skeptical implications of representationalism by insisting that the objects of knowledge *just are* the concepts (and other ideas) in an individual, collective, or divine mind.

The *grammar* of description is different in "description of facial expressions" and "description of shape, size, and color." (Compare "measuring length" and "measuring time." In learning how to use these phrases, one is learning not different applications of the same concept but different, though interrelated concepts.)

A: *Must* we use concepts to describe what we see?

B: To answer your question in the affirmative would be simply to make a grammatical remark about how our language excludes the word-formation "describing what we see without concepts."

A: What are you calling "a concept"?

B: A concept is something like a picture, model, or paradigm with which one compares objects. Although there were no concepts in the system of communication between builder and assistant described in *PI*, sec. 2, it would be easy to add to it in such a way that "slab," "block," etc. became concepts—for example, by means of a technique of describing or portraying those objects.[139]

A: Is there a sharp dividing line between language games that work with concepts and those that do not? "Concept" appears to be a vague concept!

B: The important thing is that it refers to one kind of expedient in the mechanism of language games as opposed to another.[140]

A: What about "description"? Shall we say that the orders of the builder are also descriptions?

B: Recall the "words as tools" analogy of sec. 14. If the hammer modifies the position of the nails, shall we also say that the nails modify something— the solidity of the box? And recall *PI*, sec. 24:

> If you do not keep the multiplicity of language games in view you will perhaps be inclined to ask questions like: "What is a question?"— Is it the . . . description of my mental state of uncertainty?—And is the cry "Help!" such a description?

If you do not keep the multiplicity of language games in view, you may also be inclined to say that the builder's orders are descriptions of his mental

---

139. This and the following two paragraphs are based on *RFM*, p. 433.

140. The important thing is to avoid using the word in "a typically metaphysical way, namely without an antithesis" (*BB*, p. 46).

state. And then you will need to ask yourself how assimilating the uses of words in that way could possibly make them any more like one another. For aren't they utterly unlike?[141]

The Concept of the Soul
(Part II, Section iv)

This section belongs to Wittgenstein's investigation of the concept most neglected by modern psychologists, that of the psyche or soul. I describe the larger context of this investigation later on, in "The Soulless Tribe."

"I believe my friend is suffering" is a move in a language game; "I believe he isn't an automaton" is not. Acknowledging a human being *as* human is to be contrasted with believing something *about* him, e.g., that he is really in pain and not pretending.

Is it that I'm *certain* he's human and not an automaton? How would I make certain? If I lived in an age of ersatz-human robots, I might check the back of his neck for a serial number, etc. But what would it be like to make certain the friends and neighbors I met today are human?

"I believe my friend's suffering; I *know* he's not an automaton." That is just as senseless as: "I believe babies have no teeth; I *know* roses have no teeth."[142] For what information would I convey in either case? What would one do to make certain either that roses have no teeth or that my friend is no robot? "I believe (or know) he's not an automaton," just like that, so far makes no sense.

That we react to friends (and to other human beings and certain animals) in a distinctive way is what Wittgenstein calls "an attitude towards a soul."[143] It is not what we believe or know, but what we *do*—our common reactions—that is at the bottom of the language game.[144] *Objection*: Doesn't soul talk commit one to the dubious metaphysical doctrine of dualism? *Reply*: It commits one only to a certain form of representing human experience, relations, values. *Objection*: Modern critical thinkers have no more use for the language of the soul than for the language of witches or Olympian gods. *Reply*: Consider the following lines from Wittgenstein's "Remarks on Frazer":

> [M]uch too little is made of the fact that we count the words "soul"
> and "spirit" as part of our educated vocabulary. Compared with
> this, the fact that we do not believe that our soul eats and drinks is

---

141. Compare *PI*, sec. 10 d.
142. Cf. *PI*, pp. 221–222 and sec. 420.
143. Cf. *PI*, sec. 285.
144. Compare sec. 284 b.

> a trifling matter./ If I, a person who does not believe that there are
> human-superhuman beings somewhere which one can call gods—
> if I say: "I fear the wrath of the gods," that shows that I can mean
> something by this, or can give expression to a feeling which is not
> necessarily connected with that belief. (*PO*, pp. 133, 131)[145]

Similarly, I can mean something by "What profiteth a man if he gains the
whole world and loses his soul" even if I do not believe that there are ghostly
beings somewhere that one might call "souls." Similarly, I can mean something by "The sun rises and sets" even if I do not believe the Ptolemaic theory.
Similarly:

> [I] say that I see the look that you cast at someone else. And if
> someone wanted to correct me and say that I don't really *see* it, I
> should take that for pure stupidity./ On the other hand I have not
> *made any admissions* by using that manner of speaking, and I should
> contradict anyone who told me I saw the glance "just the way" I
> see the shape and color of the eye./ For "naive language," that is to
> say our naive, normal way of expressing ourselves, does not show
> you a *theory* but only a *concept* of seeing.[146]

"But does the soul really exist?" We will want to reject that question as
nonsense once we acknowledge that "soul talk" shows us not a theory of
human life but only a concept. For then we will see its kinship with such more
obviously nonsensical questions as: "But is thought really in the head?" "Faith
really under the left nipple?"[147]

145. Wittgenstein found that Frazer's descriptions of magical-religious-metaphysical
ceremonies and turns of phrase become intelligible to us only when we see them in
relation to the very general facts about ourselves and the world "that we really know
and find interesting": "It goes without saying that a man's shadow, . . . the phenomena
of death, birth, and sexual life, in short everything we observe around us year in and
year out . . . will play a part in his thinking (his philosophy) and in his practices." (*PO*,
pp. 127–129).

146. *Z*, sec. 223. In sec. 224 Wittgenstein explains the special importance of surroundings for describing the kind of "look" somebody is giving you. (Surroundings do not
have the *same* importance when it comes to describing the color or shape of something.)

147. Cf. *PI*, sec. 589 (quoting Luther).

CHAPTER THREE

Sensation and the Soul

An intelligent way of dividing up a book on philosophy would be into parts of speech. . . . [Y]ou would have to distinguish far more parts of speech than an ordinary grammar does. You would talk for hours and hours on . . . verbs describing personal experience. We get a peculiar kind of confusion or confusions which comes up with all these words. . . . [L]anguage plays us entirely new tricks.

—*Lectures and Conversations on Aesthetics,*
Psychology, and Religious Belief, p. 1

SENSATIONS, BEETLES, AND "PRIVATE LANGUAGE"

Sensations and Beetles

What distinguishes a word from a mere noise? It is tempting to say that the essence of a word is that it *designates* something. That this is a temptation to be resisted can be brought out with the help of the tool analogy from *PI*, sec. 14. Would anything be gained by saying that the essence of a tool is to *modify* objects: the saw the length of a board—the ruler, our knowledge of its length; the hammer, the position of the nails—the nails, the solidity of the box, etc.? To say that all tools have essentially the same use just covers over potentially important differences. So too with words or (more specifically) names: it does not serve the purpose of clarity to say that all names have essentially the same use, to *designate* objects—daddy and the milk man, insects and building blocks; colors, numbers, sensations, points of the compass, etc.

In the famous "beetle in a box" passage of *PI*, sec. 293, Wittgenstein warns against construing the use of sensation words on the model of object and designation. For with this model in mind, we are liable to overlook salient facts about what kind of words "pain," "itch," "tingle," and the like *are*—for example, that we are not taught these words by being shown objects.[1]

We learned building-stone words and insect words as, at first, linguistic substitutes for pointing at things; we learned sensation and emotion words in an entirely different way. Part of the story, as Wittgenstein suggests, is that we were taught to substitute conventional expressions for natural, preverbal expressions of feeling. So the idea that names designate objects does not apply uniformly to all names. "Pain" names a sensation; by definition (as it were) a sensation is not something that can be pointed to, as can the behavior expressing it. But from this it does not follow that it names a (mysterious) inner object referred to independently of behavior.

In learning the meaning of "pain," I learned a complex concept: that one goes by what others do and say in speaking about their pains, but that one does not go by *anything* in expressing one's own feelings; that other people identify my feelings by my expressions but that I do not identify my own sensa-tions (intentions, etc.) by any criterion—I *express* them.[2] *PI*, sec. 288 speaks to this point:

> [I]f anyone said "I do not know if what I have got is a pain or some-thing else," we should think something like, he does not know what the English word "pain" means . . .

And the joke about the behaviorist who greets his colleagues every morning with the words "You feel fine. How do I feel?" underlines the point.[3]

Unlike a meaningless sound, a word is rule-governed, regulated. Someone who calls flies and ants "beetles" will be corrected for applying the word too broadly. How then is one's use of the word "pain" regulated? How do we know that we are all applying the word to the same thing?

Here the analogy with beetle talk breaks down. For while you can inspect the insects in my box to see if they are truly what you would call "bee-tles," there is nothing analogous when it comes to the sensations in my con-scious experience. So why are we so certain that we both, all too often, experience much the same unpleasant sensation when we use the word *pain*? Because the spontaneous behavior we exhibit in certain circumstances is what

---

1. My comments on *PI*, sec. 293 supplement what I say here.

2. "Express" is here replaceable by "show" or "exhibit." On "exhibiting one's pain," see *PI*, secs. 311–313 and p. 219 b.

3. A *difficulty*: why not say that "pain" has *two different meanings*—one in its first-per-son singular, present-tense use; the other in its other uses? I take up this important dif-ficulty on pp. 110–112 of "The Soulless Tribe." (Wittgenstein remarks on a parallel difficulty in *PI*, sec. 532.)

we call—what our common language entitles us to call—"the expression of pain." And so our use of "pain" to express a personal experience *does*—in its own way—get regulated: it is open to correction based on the circumstances or situations of its use. And so, for example, if your complaints of pain are just as frequently accompanied by smiles and giggles as by moans and groans, we will rightly doubt your grasp of the meaning of the word "pain."[4]

How does one learn the meaning of "pain"? Is it by learning the conventional name for what you feel when you hit your thumb with a hammer, and the like?

> When one learns to use the word "pain," that does not happen through guessing which of the inner processes connected with falling down, etc. this word is used for./ For in that case [the patently nonsensical] problem might arise . . . : on account of *which* of my sensations do I cry out when I damage myself?/ And here I imagine one's pointing inside and asking himself: "Is it *this* sensation, or *this* one?" (*RPP*-I, sec. 305)

There is such a thing as teaching someone what a dung beetle is by pointing to a specimen and saying, "*That's* a dung beetle"; there is no such thing as teaching someone what pain is by "getting him to point inward to something when he falls, etc." and saying, "*That's* pain."[5]

Suppose we acknowledge that "pain" and other names for psychological states ("fear," "understanding," "intention," etc.) are not in fact learned by learning to recognize an inner something on the basis of a private ostensive definition. We might still feel that there *could* be a word learned in that way—a feeling that (as we saw) Wittgenstein investigates by imagining that he is a diarist wanting to keep a record of the recurrence of a certain sensation:

> To this end I associate it with the sign "S" . . . and at the same time concentrate my attention on the sensation—and so, as it were, point to it inwardly. (*PI*, sec. 258)

Referring to this "diarist's" procedure as a *ceremony* (*Zeremonie*, formality), Wittgenstein implies that he has not succeeded in naming anything. "Can one *within oneself* attach a name to a sensation?" he asks in *RPP*-I, sec. 306:

> What happens here; and what is the result of this action? . . . If one shuts a door in one's mind, is it then shut? And what are the consequences? That, in one's mind, now no one can get in?[6]

---

4. Based on *RPP*-I, sec. 304.

5. This is not to say that we could not teach an adult foreigner the English word for pain by a kind of ostensive definition. See *PI*, sec. 288.

6. Cf. *PI*, secs. 259–268.

If I am under orders to keep the door in my mind shut, how am I to know if I obey or disobey? Here, as in the case of the "diarist," I have no criterion of correctness. "Whatever is going to seem obedience to me *is* obedience." But that only means that here we cannot talk about "obedience."

The diarist is suffering from an illusion. His "S-game" does not really serve as a means of communicating with himself about the recurrence of a certain sensation, S. For no criterion of identity has been determined in his game for S: no sense established for judgments of the form "Yes, it's the same sensation again," and "No, it's a different one."

"Surely there is *something* about an individual's feelings that cannot be put into words?" Wittgenstein would not want to deny it. What he wants is to reject a certain word formation, namely: "language in which I can describe for my own benefit states of affairs that in principle can't be communicated to anyone else." He wants us to see that there is no use for that word formation in our language—and that we do not want to give it one.

If you think you want to give it a use, Wittgenstein would ask you to explain what sort of thing you're tempted to call "privately but not publicly communicable." Suppose you say that you want to describe the *exact degree* of someone else's pain in that way. Wittgenstein considers—and gently ridicules—that suggestion in *Zettel*, sec. 536:

> "I may know that he is in pain, but I never know the exact degree of his pain. So here is something that he knows and that his expression of pain does not tell me. Something purely private." He knows exactly how severe his pain is? Isn't that much as if one were to say he always knows exactly where he is? Namely here. Is the concept of degree given with the pain?[7]

We do not learn the concept of intense pain by *having* intense pains. We learn it by learning the use of "intense pain" and related words in the language. And these words are public property. I do not know the intensity of *my* pains in an incommunicably exact way just because they are my pains any more than I know my location in some incommunicably precise sense just because I am *here*.

How Private Can You Get?

"Can you be *sure* that there can't be a private language?," asks the critic. Wittgenstein's response is to *question* this insistent philosophical question, by asking what it would be for a language to be private in the desired sense. How about a secret code such as the one Samuel Pepys invented for his diary?

---

7. I have modified the punctuation of the text a bit.

Would that do? No; that's certainly not the kind of thing the philosophers had in mind. So we need to imagine something else.

"We could even imagine human beings who spoke only in monologue; who accompanied their activities by talking to themselves" (*PI*, sec. 243). Although these speakers would not be communicating amongst themselves or with us, we might still come to understand what they were saying to themselves:

> An explorer who watched them and listened to their talk might succeed in translating their language into ours. (This would enable him to predict these people's actions correctly, for he also hears them making resolutions and decisions.) (ibid)

Imagine now that we accompany the explorer to another country and find people who carry on the usual human activities and in the course of them seem to employ an articulate language:

> If we watch their behavior . . . it seems "logical." But when we try to learn their language, we find it impossible to do so. For there is no regular connection between what they say, the sounds they make, and their actions; but still these sounds are not superfluous, for if we gag one of the people, it has the same consequences as with us; without the sounds their actions fall into confusion . . . (*PI*, sec. 207)

But do the actions of these people and the sounds they make belong in the company of what we call "*language* games"—along with giving and obeying orders, describing the appearance of an object, etc.? No. There is not enough regularity for us to call what they are doing *language*. (Just as not everything that looks like a key and can be used to open a lock *is* a key, so not everything that sounds like and has the consequences of language *is* language.[8])

"[S]ounds which no one else understands but which I '*appear to understand*' might be called a 'private language'" (*PI*, sec. 269). But would there be any point in digging in our heels and insisting on referring to such "logical" but untranslatable sounds as "a private language"? Is *that* the sort of thing we, or "the private diarist," were looking for?

We shall try to imagine something deeper—"the privacy of the soul's dialogue with itself." The point of *this* private language would be to enable us to give expression to our innermost experiences for our own private use.

> Well, can't we do so in our ordinary language?—But that is not what I mean. The individual words of *this* language are to refer to

---

8. On the lock-and-key analogy, see *WLG*, pp. 17–18, 135–136, and 257.

what can only be known to the person speaking; to his immediate
private sensations. So another person cannot understand the language. (*PI*, sec. 243; my emphasis.)

It was in sec. 258, "the diary passage," that Wittgenstein's exploration of this
suggestion came to a head. His argument was that the diarist had not really
named anything because he had provided no way of distinguishing "using 'S'
in accordance with the rule he'd established" from "*just thinking* he was." His
"S-game" stands in sharp contrast to the everyday language games in which

there are certain criteria in a man's behavior for the fact that he
does not understand a word. . . . And criteria for his "thinking he
understands," attaching some meaning to the word, but not the
right one. And, lastly, criteria for his understanding the word
right. (*PI*, sec. 269)

Now is there anything more than a superficial resemblance between the
diarist's S-game and our everyday practice of language? Compare the following case from *PI*, sec. 653:

I tell someone that I walked a certain route, going by a map which
I had prepared beforehand. Thereupon I show him the map, and it
consists of lines on a piece of paper; but I cannot explain how these
lines are the map of my movements. . . . Yet I did follow the drawing with all the characteristic tokens of reading a map.

Calling what the diarist did with S "using a private name" might be put to
much the same use as calling the practice just described "following a private
map"—in a joke.

Seeing Red Blue

Samples figure in the use of color words as they do not in the use of words for
pain, tingle, and other bodily sensations. But what if we experience different
color sensations when viewing the same color sample?

[S]omeone says "I can't understand it, I see everything red blue
today, and vice versa." We answer "It must look queer!" He says it
does, and, e.g., goes on to say how cold the glowing coal looks and
how warm the clear blue sky. I think we should under these or similar circumstances be inclined to say that he saw red what we saw
blue. (*PO*, p. 231)[9]

Suppose we go further and say that someone might *always* see as red what the
rest of us call blue. That would have the effect of prying the color words from
their connection with color samples. Nor would it help to speak of "pointing

---

9. From "Notes for Lectures on 'Private Experience' and 'Sense Data'" (1934–36).

inwardly to private color samples." For color words are common property and defined in terms of samples we can all point to.[10]

We need to distinguish two importantly different uses of color samples:

> [1] If you don't see this chair and I wish to describe its color, I say "The chair is like this" and point to a sample. [2] . . . in a psychological experiment: a current is sent through you and you are asked to say what colors you see. You might answer . . . [by] just pointing to a colored patch. (*PO*, p. 346)[11]

We are tempted to imagine that in the psychological experiment there is also a patch you *cannot* point to, a "private object":

> Generally if I point to a sample there's a way of checking whether I am right or wrong. [But] it is different in the psychological experiment, where I can't point to anything. This is not because I can't open my inside. There isn't anything to point to. (ibid., p. 346)

This is a rejection not of the psychological facts but of a misleading way of picturing them. The picture is that of the subject's *looking* at something with his mind's eye and matching it with the (external) sample. It is misleading because it suggests that the subject points to the sample *because* it matches his impression—which is wrong, since saying, "This sample matches the impression before my mind's eye," is logically equivalent to just pointing to the sample. It merely adds a picturesque ornamentation.

"I know how red looks to me." But does saying, "I *know* it looks blue to me," mean anything more than "It looks blue to me"? Knowing implies justification but here there is none. I can justify "The car is beet red" by producing a sample of beet red (e.g., a beet); there is no comparable procedure for "I am seeing red blue." I can *explain* how the coals look to me by saying "beet red," or by pointing to a standard sample, but I am not thereby *justifying* my statement. If I took seriously requests that I justify my own reports of how things look to me, that would suggest linguistic ignorance or mental confusion on my part.

Although I neither have nor lack justification for saying, "I see red blue," there *is* something that regulates my use of that language.[12] If I am to use "seeing red blue" meaningfully, I must already have mastered color talk, which requires that I be in general agreement with others in my color predications.

---

10. Cf. *PI*, sec. 261, and *PO*, p. 342 ("If by 'pain' we mean something *private*, then we ought not to say it means a certain *feeling* . . . ")

11. This and the following quotation are from notes taken by Rush Rhees of Wittgenstein's 1936 lectures.

12. Cf. *PI*, secs. 289 and 357.

And I must *limit* that use: if I routinely speak of seeing red blue or claim I've always seen it that way, you will rightly wonder what, if anything, I mean.

THE SOULLESS TRIBE

> Speculation. A tribe that we have brought into subjection, which we want to make into a slave race. . . . The government and the scientists give it out that the people of this tribe have no souls; so they can be used without scruple for any purpose whatever. (*RPP-*I, secs. 93 and 96)

> When the slaves say something happens in them, . . . does this confirm that they have souls? . . . If they say now "something happens in my head— my soul—" that only shows that they use a certain picture. (*WLG*, pp. 42-43)

My title derives from these and other remarks in which Wittgenstein develops the fiction of "a soulless tribe." What is its significance?

In notes for a 1936 lecture, Wittgenstein says that when a man moans with pain, "there is nothing *behind* the moaning" (*PO*, p. 262). Was he putting us on a level with his "soulless tribe"? Is there truth in the common impression that he denied the inner life? This section is an effort to clarify the passages on the soulless tribe and at the same time challenge the common impression that Wittgenstein "left something out" in his philosophy of psychology.[13] I have drawn on material dating from 1935 to 1951 and tried to weave it into a smooth, perspicuous whole. The resulting account seems to me more "the completion of a Gestalt" than the exposition of a doctrine.[14]

Pain and Its Expression

To speak of pain as "behind the pain behavior," or of thought as "in the soul," is not to say something false. But it does slur over categorical differences, differences revealed only by close attention to actual word use. Projecting everything into "the inner" evades the difficulty of describing the *field* of our language. So we end up with "explanations" that get us nowhere.

There are people in pain, and people behaving as though they are when they're not. This difference is not to be explained by saying that there is a cer-

---

13. Iris Murdoch speaks of an "unbearable narrowness in Wittgenstein's use of the image of outer criteria" (*Metaphysics*, p. 275). José Benardete speaks of "the widespread impression that at the heart of *PI* lies a profound darkness," tracing this "darkness" to an unresolved tension between wanting and not wanting to allow factual reference to "pain" (*Philosophical Studies* 72 [1993], pp. 279–280).

14. The account to follow is an abbreviated version of an article I published in 1995. Many of the numerous textual references have been omitted.

tain something behind the behavior of the people really in pain. For if instead of saying "a certain something" one is bold enough to say *pain*, then the "explanation's" tautologous character would be manifest.[15]

I can certainly confess that I was simulating pain—confess an intention to deceive others about how I feel. But since this possibility of confession is what "in my consciousness" consists in here, one does not explain "in my consciousness" in terms of it. And although someone who has been keeping his feelings to himself may later reveal his inmost heart to us by a confession, this fact provides no "proof of the existence of the inner." Anyone who needed such a proof would have to dismiss the "confession" on the grounds that it *too* is something outer.[16]

What makes me certain that so-and-so's confession is sincere, or that his pain is real, may not make you certain.[17] The existence of such stubborn disagreements between people is not *explained* by saying that their inner worlds are closed to each other. Rather, we *describe* the disagreement by using that picture. (Not: objective certainty is lacking *because* we don't see into their souls. But: "we don't see into their souls" = "objective certainty is lacking.")

Lying implies an intention to deceive. And intention, we say, is something inner. But how do we know this? It would be circular to answer, "We verify it introspectively." That intentions, pains, etc. are inner is not a verifiable description—not a proposition that may or may not be supported by evidence; it is a grammatical remark—an effort to bring out something about the use of "intention," "pain," etc.

"Pain is to moaning what the contents of a box are to its outward appearance." This comparison is not empirical in the way that (for instance) "Gills are to fish what lungs are to dogs" is empirical. That does not make it arbitrary, however, in the sense of pointless. For comparing pain, intention, etc. to items in a sealed box can vividly express significant points of grammar: the points that our language game contains "logical space" for doubting another's avowals of pain, intention, etc., and that it does not contain criteria sufficient to resolve every disagreement about another's avowal of pain, etc.

Can someone under anaesthesia experience pain? We sometimes acknowledge groaning (or something else) as a criterion for answering this

---

15. Based on *PO*, p. 449. Cf. *LW-I*, sec. 975: Saying, "My feelings are inaccessible to him because they take place within my consciousness," would also be tautologous: it would be just another way of saying, "They're inaccessible."

16. Based on *RPP-II*, sec. 703. Cf. *PI*, p. 223.

17. *LW-II*, p. 21: "'I am *certain* that he's in pain.' . . . [W]hat *makes* us certain? Not a proof. That is, what makes me certain doesn't make someone else certain." Cf. *PI*, p. 227.

question, sometimes not. But the language game without criteria presupposes the language game with criteria. (Lytton Strachey reports trying to imagine Queen Victoria's last thoughts as she lay dying. To say he was guessing her thoughts would be a secondary use of the word: it presupposes the language game in which there is a criterion for "guessing right" as opposed to "guessing wrong.")[18]

The importance of expression to our concept of pain comes to light in the following series:

a) One person has a toothache for one minute but doesn't show it.
b) Two people have toothaches for two minutes but don't show it.
c) N people have toothaches for n minutes but don't show it.
d) All people have toothaches all the time but don't show it.[19]

The fact that we do not see "d" as a continuation of the series shows that expression belongs to the *concept* of pain. The importance of the concept in our lives is shown by the fact that we neither have a use for "d" nor want to give it one.

If we see someone writhing in pain with evident cause, we react to her suffering, *do* something. We don't think: "Her feelings are *hidden* from us." So disagreements in judgment about the feelings of others have their limits.[20]

"How can we be *certain* that the 'sufferer' is not dissembling in even the 'most evident' cases?" We do not look to a knowledge of human nature for an answer to this question. For we have no clear idea of what it is supposed to mean, no clear idea of what we would count as an answer to it. It is, therefore, the "question" that needs grounding, rather than the "certainty" it challenges.

The question is perhaps reflective of—and so in a sense grounded on— an elementary point of grammar, namely that there is room for dissembling in our language game. Thus: "You may lose at this game" may say no more than that in *this* situation, in contrast to when we're "just playing around," there is such a thing as losing and winning. Similarly: "A person may always be lying" may say no more than that there is such a thing as lying and truthfulness in the language game between us, in contrast to very primitive forms of the game.

Suppose people seldom admitted what they were thinking. That would not affect the grammatical point that thinking-but-not-admitting is an "exception concept." It can only be explained to someone who already understands "thinking and admitting." (Compare "calculating in the head": a sec-

---

18. See *WLG*, pp. 32, 274. For "under anaesthesia," see *RPP*-II, sec. 645.

19. From unpublished notes by Margaret Macdonald on 1935–1936 lectures by Wittgenstein on personal experience. With thanks to Cora Diamond.

20. See *PI*, sec. 420.

ondary use of "calculating," this must be explained in terms of "calculating on paper" or the like.)

"When you think something but do not admit it, no outward expression accompanies your inner thought; when you think something and admit it, some outward expression does accompany your thought." But that is only to redescribe the concept, not to provide another (more direct) way of explaining it.

"What happens when someone has a toothache?" A philosopher might answer: "Something is going on in his tooth and, accompanying that, something in his consciousness—something dreadful." But this answer—this philosophical analysis, as we might call it—gets us no further than the shorter and patently tautological answer: "He's having a toothache!"

Although the "pain-with-accompanying-behavior picture" creates no problems for us in everyday life, it does create problems for us when we stand back and reflect on it. For then a case like "fever accompanying an infection" comes to mind and we try to make *it* our paradigm of accompaniment. We end up misconstruing the grammar of the expression of pain by forcing it into that mold. For although one can say: "I have a fever; infection and fever go together; so I have an infection," one cannot say: "I'm exhibiting pain behavior; pain behavior and pain go together; so I'm in pain."

"'Feigning pain' = 'pain behavior unaccompanied by pain.'" That equation gives us a picture—one we can use or not use. While we are inclined to think of malingering as pain behavior minus something—pain—we *could* think of it as pain behavior plus something—a dishonest purpose.

Wittgenstein's philosophical colleague C. D. Broad once said of a man complaining of toothache: "Perhaps nothing happens in his mind when he says he has it; but certainly when I sympathize with him, I believe that something does" (WLG, p. 284). That makes the sympathy for the sufferer sound quite separate and distinct from the belief he is in pain. Why not call the sympathy a *form* of the belief? "Pity, one may say, is a form of conviction that someone else is in pain" (PI, sec. 287).

"'We *see* emotion.'—As opposed to what?—We do not see facial contortions and make inferences from them (like a doctor framing a diagnosis) to joy, grief, boredom. We describe a face immediately as sad, radiant, bored, even when we are unable to give any other description of the features" (Z, sec. 225). Noel Fleming glossed that oft-quoted passage as follows:

> To see the joy in someone's face is not to interpret some outward signs by accepting an hypothesis about his inner life. . . . What it is to do, much more, is to react to him in a certain way. . . .[21]

---

21. "Seeing the Soul," *Philosophy* (1978), p. 37.

This is all right as long as the "reaction" is understood as *cognitive*—a form of conviction that someone feels joy.

Rejoicing-with, jealousy, pity, and so forth: these make my attitude toward another "an attitude towards a soul" (*PI*, p. 178). So there must be something wrong with Fleming's idea that the soul, for Wittgenstein, is no more than "the body itself making faces and moving around" (p. 43). For when we (for example) pity someone, we are not pitying his *body* (*PI*, sec. 286). And to characterize someone as "a body making faces and moving around" would suggest an attitude far removed from "an attitude towards a soul"!22

The language game in which we formulate beliefs and doubts about the suffering of others is founded on spontaneous reactions:

> [I]t is a primitive reaction to tend, to treat, the part that hurts
> when someone else is in pain; and not merely when oneself is—
> and so to pay attention to other people's pain-behavior, as one
> does *not* pay attention to one's own pain behavior./ But what is the
> word "primitive" meant to say here? Presumably that this sort of
> behavior is *pre-linguistic*: that a language game is based *on it*, that it
> is the prototype of a way of thinking and not the result of thought.
> (Z, secs. 540-541.)

"Certain kinds of prelinguistic behavior are foundational": in child psychology this sentence would function as an empirical hypothesis; in this philosophical context it is meant to bring out a conceptual point. Compare *PI*, sec. 244:

> How do words *refer* to sensations? . . . Here is one possibility: words
> are connected with the primitive, the natural, expressions of the
> sensation and used in their place.

That *this* is a possibility tells us something about the kind of word *pain* (for example) is. It tells us that if *that* is how it might have been learned, then it's certainly not (for example) a number, color, or thing word.

Asymmetry

"Feeling, "thinking," and other psychological words are united by a certain asymmetry between the first-person singular, present-tense use and all other uses. The question "Am I thinking of chicken?," for example, does not make

---

22. Cf. *RPP-II*, sec. 690: "Am I saying something like, 'and the soul itself is merely something about the body'? No. (I am not that hard up for categories.)" In "Loosing Your Concepts," Cora Diamond explores the fact that many modern thinkers *are* "that hard up for categories."

the same sort of sense as "Are you thinking of chicken?" There is no comparable asymmetry in the use of nonpsychological verbs: "Am I eating chicken?,"
for example, *does* make the same sort of sense as "Are you eating chicken?"

This asymmetry makes it look as if "thinking" means one thing in its
first-person use and something else in its other-person use. Why does it exist?
What, if anything, is its importance?

Recalling the place of thinking (believing, etc.) in our life, we see that
the grammar of the first-person expression of thought mirrors a fact that is
enormously important for us: that we do not normally infer our own beliefs
from our own behavior. So we would find it ludicrous to hear someone say: "I
must think someone's at the door, judging from the way I'm moving toward
it."

Recall the place of sensations and emotions in our life. Our children
learn to use the word *pain* of other people on the basis of observing them, and
the same word of themselves without observing anybody. Suppose we found a
language in which one word was used for the first person and a different word
for the third: this fact would be of no special interest to us once we learned
the translation. The causes and consequences of pain, alleviation of pain and
compassion for the sufferer: *these* are always of special interest to us.

Just as "I have a toothache" can stand in for a moan of complaint,
though it does not *mean* "I moan," so too "He has a toothache" can stand in for
a moan of compassion (as it were), though it does not *mean* "I feel sorry for
him." This is the sort of everyday fact that helps disclose how the first- and
third-person uses go together. One might add that the first- and the third-person utterances refer to the same object: the first from a privileged "inner" vantage point; the third from an indirect, "external" vantage point. Presented as
an explanation or analysis, this addition would just obfuscate matters. But it
does need to be presented—as a picture. And then we will have to investigate
the kind of role it has in our lives.

"I can take another man's word for his beliefs but cannot take my word
for my own beliefs." Isn't that just arbitrary? *No.* Certain facts about psychological phenomena correspond to the asymmetry that runs through the psychological words; therefore, it is not just arbitrary.[23] But these facts seem more
trivial and humdrum than we might have expected—facts such as:

1) It doesn't happen often that I guess your thoughts.

---

23. Compare "I can show you reddish blue but not reddish green." Isn't *that* just arbitrary? Couldn't someone be trained to call *olive* "reddish green," and doesn't that show
that "It's only how we look at it"? No. Language games *do* have foundations—only not
of a kind we are inclined to expect. (See *WLG*, p. 258 and "Color Grammar," below.)

> [T]here *is* something "private": we don't often guess Smith's
> thoughts. . . . It *could* have been that everybody always murmurs
> and that many have a knack for reading murmurs. (WLG, pp.
> 275–277, my emphasis)

2) It hasn't come to pass that whenever a man "adds in his head" we can
observe his larynx and reliably predict the sum he will come out with. If it
did, the idea of an inner calculation would lose its point.[24]

3) One cannot observe oneself as one does someone else.

> I *can* not observe myself as I do someone else, cannot ask myself
> "What is this person likely to do now?" etc./ Therefore the verb
> "He believes," "I believed" *can* not have the kind of continuation
> in the first person as the verb "to eat."/ . . . "But what *would* the
> continuation be that I was expecting?!" I can see none. (LW-II, p.
> 10)

4) I don't bother about my own groaning, as I often do about another person's.

> I infer that he needs to go to the doctor from observation of his
> behavior; but I do *not* make this inference in my own case from
> observation of my behavior. Or rather: I do this too sometimes, but
> *not* in parallel cases. (Z, sec. 539)

Pain, thought, and other elementary psychological concepts are closely interwoven with these and other facts of living—so closely that no legislator could
abolish them.

"The Soulless Tribe"

We now return to the fiction from which we began.

To say of a people that they have no souls might be part of an effort to
enslave them. These "soulless ones" might even prove useful as experimental
subjects in psychological laboratories since their reactions, including their linguistic reactions, are quite those of their "soul-endowed" masters.

Suppose we are the masters. We have much the same use for the sentence "I believe he has a toothache" when talking of our slaves as we do when
speaking of ourselves. This sameness of use is reflected in the fact that our criteria for applying the sentence are the same. Although we react differently
(have been trained to react differently) when applying the sentence to a "soulless one" than when applying it to one of our own, *what we go by* in applying it
is quite the same. We react to our slaves as if they were automata rather than
living human beings. If one screams and writhes, we regard him as we would a
machine that needs to be fixed or replaced. The more mechanical a slave

---

24. Based on WLG, pp. 275–276.

appears to us, the easier we find it to regard him in this way. ("The opposite of being full of soul is being mechanical" [*RPP*-I, sec. 324].)

Suppose we happen to notice in one of our slaves a (as it were) "suffering expression" or (alternatively) a "cunning, deceitful look": now we feel that he has become "transparent to us," that we are "looking into him." This might make us stop regarding him as soulless. If so, what would this change in us amount to? It would *not* be a matter of hypothesizing an "inner cause" and believing that *it* explains the complicated play of expressions, etc. that we observed in him:

> Feigning and its opposite exist only when there is a compli-
> cated *play of expressions*. (Just as false or correct moves exist
> only *in a game*.) And if the play of *expression* develops, then
> indeed I can say that a soul, something *inner*, is developing.
> But now the inner is no longer the cause {the prime mover}
> of the expression. (No more than mathematical thinking
> produces calculations, or is the impetus behind them. . . .)[25]

Should we change our habitual attitude toward a slave from one of cold calculation to one of sympathetic concern, we would also change our way of representing him to ourselves. We would then find it natural to speak of "what he has in mind" and of his "mental arithmetic," for example. We might even picture his death as a ghost leaving a recumbent body, as perhaps now we picture the death of our own. All this would express a radical change of attitude. Our attitude toward him will now be "an attitude toward a soul,"—an attitude toward a human.

I am not of the *opinion* that someone is not an automaton. But what is the difference between an attitude and an opinion? I might be of the opinion that human beings are automata (having heard it in a physiology class) without its influencing my attitude toward all human beings. (I might even come to believe that I, too, am a machine, without its affecting my attitude toward myself.)

> I would like to say: the attitude comes *before* the opinion. . . . / How
> would this be: only one who can utter it as information *believes* it?/
> An opinion can be wrong. But what would an error look like
> here?[26]

---

25. *LW*-I, secs. 946–947. ("{ }" enclose an alternate phrasing in the text.) On "transparent to us," see *LW*-II, p. 67.
26. *LW*-II, p. 38. Compare OC, secs 23, 622, where it is suggested that propositions such as "I am a human being" and "The earth has existed for a very long time" show us the hardest layers of the "river bed" of our thought and action. If the certainty of "I

In circumstances in which they would say of one of their own that she's calculating in her head (for example), the slave owners would not say the same of a slave. When a visiting foreigner exclaims that something *must* be going on in her, something *inner*, he is ridiculed as sentimental, superstitious, and stupid. To the objection that surely the slaves' notorious malingering *proves* they have some sort of inner life, the reply is that this "malingering" is not a conscious effort to deceive, but merely their sometimes giving pain signals without the usual antecedents and consequents. But suppose they spontaneously come out with things like "something happens *in* us when. . . . " To the question whether this new behavior is evidence that perhaps something *is* happening in them, we reply with a parallel but obviously nonsensical question such as: "Would the fact that our children begin spontaneously to call low notes 'dark' be evidence that perhaps low notes *are* dark?"

Why do we have the concepts we do? Compare "We have the concept 'dark note' because there *are* such notes" with "We have the concept 'irrational number' because there *are* such numbers." These answers are of course unhelpful; in this they are alike. They differ in that the second is about a weightier concept than the first. The concept of an irrational number is connected with our interests and activities; our interests and activities are connected with particular facts of everyday living. We have to pay attention to such interests, activities, and facts if we are to respond helpfully to the initial question; for it is by attending to *them* that we are reminded of the point of our concepts, i.e., of the kind of role they have in our lives.

The masters see to it that the children of the slaves are trained in the use of the same concepts as are their own children. Yet they habitually regard their slaves as automata, and train their children to do likewise. Is there some fact of the matter they are overlooking? No. They can see as well as anyone else that the slaves are men, women, and children who look, act, and live much like themselves. It is just that they make a practice of not acknowledging their humanity. This practice shows us something about *them*. What it shows is not factual or linguistic error, but (as we might put it) a certain constriction of soul. (But isn't this soul talk misleading?

> So little misleading, that it is quite intelligible if I say "My soul is tired, not just my mind." But don't you at least say that everything that can be expressed by means of the word "soul" can also be expressed somehow by means of words for the corporeal? I do not say that. But if it were so—what would it amount to? For the words, and also what we point to in explaining them, are nothing

---

have two hands" is not as "hard," that's because we *do* know what an error would look like there.

but instruments, and everything depends on their use. [*RPP-I*, sec. 586; cf. II-690])

Compare "slave owners who insist that their slaves are really automata" with "window manufacturers who insist that German-made windows are really without true cross pieces." These manufacturers always see the cross-pieces in German windows as swastikas, and train their workers always to refer to them as such.

> But can't I imagine that the people around me are automata, lack consciousness, even though they behave in the same way as usual? . . . [J]ust try to keep hold of this idea in the midst of your ordinary intercourse with others . . . !/ Seeing a living human being as an automaton is analogous to seeing one figure as a limiting case or variant of another; the cross pieces of a window as a swastika, for example. (*PI*, sec. 420)

Contrary to Noel Fleming and other critics, Wittgenstein is not reducing "having a soul" to "being seen as having a soul." When Wittgenstein talks about seeing human beings as automata (and therefore soulless), he is talking about a secondary use of the word. In its primary use, "automata" has no application to human beings. If, then, someone calls a human being "an automaton," and this is not just a verbal slip or a "parroting of what the teacher said," then he is using that combination of words to express something—a reaction or an attitude. Similarly, if someone calls a sound bright or dark, that may reveal a weak grasp of English, or a misunderstanding, or it may express a certain (more or less personal) reaction to the sound.

"Pain" is ascribed primarily to human beings and other living creatures, secondarily to dolls and other inanimate things; secondary pain ascriptions are not correct or mistaken, as are the primary pain ascriptions.[27] A slave master who insists that his slaves are really automata is no more guilty of stupidity and mistake than is a child who ascribes pain to her dolls and pities them; it is just that his behavior is expressive of a sinister and far less innocent soul.

In its "ideal" form, the slave owner's attitude toward his slaves is radically and relentlessly different from his attitude toward himself and "his kind." It is an attitude rooted not in an *opinion* but a *form of life*.

The Picture of the Inner

Compare the uses of "thinking," "believing," "sensing," "feeling" with their associated picture. While the *uses* are many and complex, the *picture* is of

---

27. "Here one might speak of a 'primary' and a 'secondary' sense of a word. It is only if the word has the primary sense for you that you use it in the secondary one" (*PI*, p. 216).

something unitary and simple in which invisible activities are taking place. The story of the soulless tribe is meant to show that this picture is like a pair of glasses on our nose—something we can "take off."

While it is neither possible nor desirable to do without "the picture of the inner" or "idea of the soul" in our language and our lives, it *is* possible and desirable to abstract from them when we need to analyze psychological concepts. In that context of analysis, the story of the soulless tribe functions not in a description of a hateful ideology but as an "auxiliary construction" in a process of clarifying the use of psychological predicates in our lives. It helps us represent the variety and complexity of that use.

"Soulless tribesmen" are taught something like a signal game with psychological terms such as "I'm in pain" and "I'm depressed." In the case of pain, they are trained to substitute a language gesture for the primitive gesture of "pointing to where it hurts"; there is nothing comparable in the case of depression. "I'm in pain" is attached to certain local reactions, such as nursing an injured knee; there is nothing like this in "I'm depressed." And, though both expressions are important to us regarding future behavior, they are not important in the same way. If, in the end, we are persuaded to speak of the tribesmen as experiencing both pain and depression "within themselves," then the expressions of pain and depression begin look alike. "The picture of the inner" puts a face of unity over an underlying diversity.

When we move back from our close look at the underlying diversity, the "face of unity" reemerges. "[W]e cannot get away from forming the picture of a mental process."[28] Why? "*Not* because we are acquainted with it in our own case!" Why then?

> We combine diverse elements into a "Gestalt" (pattern), for example, into one of deceit./ The picture of the inner completes the Gestalt. (RPP-II, sec. 651)

Professor Cora Diamond makes the clarifying suggestion that "the diverse elements being combined into the pattern of deceit might be behavior, utterances, a certain intelligence, a look in someone's eyes." They are combined, she adds,

> by the fact that I can see the diverse things as together forming a pattern, the pattern of deceit. I think of the pattern as completed by an inner intention, the intention to deceive: the completion of

---

28. This and the following quoted sentence are from *RPP-II*, sec. 668.

> the pattern in this way helps me to construe the other disparate
> items as belonging to a pattern.[29]

Yesterday I was told that N was smiling and cheerful, today that he's still cheerful but no longer smiling. I combine these and other diverse facts and impressions into the Gestalt of deceit. To complete the Gestalt, I picture an inwardly smiling N wearing a mask of depression or of pain—so that less will be demanded of him today.

Think back to the first-/third-person asymmetry. Diverse psychological phenomena are united by this one property. But does each psychological predicate have two meanings: one in its first-, another in its third-person use? No. What I identify on the basis of another's cries and moans is the very same state he simply expresses in those cries and moans. But what is this thing that I identify and he expresses? Not something over-against-us that either one of us can point at; something inner. ("The picture of the inner" here again unifies a diversity.)

"*I* say you're in pain because I hear your groans; *you* don't say you're in pain for the same reason. Can we really mean the same by 'pain'?"—What kind of question is that?

> The question can be raised: Is a state that I recognize on the basis
> of someone's utterances really the same as the state he does not
> recognize this way? And the answer is a decision. (LW-II, pp. 8–9)

Suppose I'm a slave owner who has finally come to see the humanity in a slave. Perhaps I see him injured and react with a sympathetic "I know how it must feel!" (I might have hardened my heart.) I have thereby identified "what *I* recognize on the basis of observing his injury and hearing his cries" with "what *he has* but does not recognize in that way." I have thereby placed what I recognize in him in the same box with what *I* have when I'm injured—the box marked "psychological—inner—reality." I now not only use the same word, *pain*, of his state and mine when we are injured and crying out; I also apply the same picture to them: "states of mind," "passions of the soul." In extending application of the picture in this way, I express my acknowledgment of his humanity. ("And the answer is a decision." Yes, I made a decision—to *do* something, to apply the picture of the soul to the man. I didn't: "decide that he has a soul." That means nothing.)

"It does seem as though what *I* recognize and *he* expresses is the same." But this is a picture, not something that *seems* to be so.[30] What we do with this

---

29. From a letter to me dated November 30, 1994.

30. Compare *PI*, p. 184 d.

picture is to express a certain attitude and to pass it along to our children: "an attitude toward a soul." It is important to pass along this attitude to our children because of its foundational role in their moral education. This service to moral education is part of what gives "the picture of the inner" its meaning.

"The pain I recognize and he expresses is the same; the pain I express and he recognizes is the same." One learns the picture of the inner in the course of learning these asymmetries. Such learning (I want to say) provides soil on which seeds of morality can sprout and grow—"seeds" such as the Golden Rule.[31]

Abusing the Picture

We say that pain is a sensation, but we cannot justify this by reference to a noticeable similarity between pains and other things we call "sensations"— itches, smells, sounds, color impressions, etc. The similarity must be in the concept; so it must be grammar, not experience, that tells us what kind of object pain is.

Kinds of numbers have formal properties in common but differ in their application.[32] Similarly, although nothing could be more unlike than meters and minutes, they share a formal property—they are both measures.

Although the terms *believes, intends, in pain,* etc., differ enormously in their application, they (and the other psychological predicates) have in common that, in their first-person singular, present-tense use, doubt and the possibility of mistake are ruled out. We may call the indubitability and incorrigibility involved here a property (or conjunction of properties) so long as we realize that in doing so we are making not a *material* but a *formal* point. For we are not here predicating something of something else—any more than we were when we said that 2 and 4 are numbers, or when we said that meters and minutes are measures. To "predicate a formal property" is to make a grammatical remark. It is to characterize a language game rather than to "make a move in it."

Whatever characterizes a language game belongs to grammar. But grammar, as it is of interest to philosophy, cannot always be *equated* with rules (criteria, techniques) for the employment of words. We can see this with the help of our story about the slave masters in relation to their slaves: although they

---

31. CV, pp. 1a, 30d, and 49b seem relevant to this topic, as does the second Edelman paper mentioned in the bibliography (which connects the question about the authority of moral judgments with "a kind of concern one might have for others *as* human" [p. 342].)

32. What "formal property" is in the *Tractatus*, "place or station in grammar" is in the *Investigations*.

did not alter its rules, their language game with the psychological words had a different *sense* for them when they extended it from themselves to their slaves. So bringing out the sense of a language game is not the same as tabulating its rules.[33] We also, in the present case, need to imagine how "the picture of the inner" might have been used *and abused* by those who taught us the language game with the psychological words.

Like everyone else, I was taught as a child to say, "He's in pain," as well as, "I'm in pain"; also that pain is pain, whether it is mine or his. I learned (in effect) that although pain is something we both feel, it is not like the kitten we can both feel together: it is subjective or inner, not over-against-us or outer; it is private not public—nobody can know my pains unless I show them. I learned that pain, although subjective, is nonetheless real; and that, although private, it can—in its own way—be shown.

I imagine that had I been born into the slaveholding community, I might have been "informed" at a certain age that—properly speaking—people can only show *signs* of their sensations, and trained to ridicule the idea that they really ever show their *sensations*.[34] I might then have been informed of what "the wisest scientists and philosophers" have concluded about our slaves: that their cries and groans are not, as with us, ever signs of an inner, psychological reality; that, with them, cries and groans are no more than signals of an external, mechanical malfunction.

Conclusion

The picture of the inner belongs to "the mythology stored in our language."[35] Is it an ornament—like a king's paper crown in the *Blue Book* chess game?[36] It is too firmly rooted in us and in the facts of our life to be called that. Is it a

---

33. Cf. *PI*, sec. 282: "(When children play at trains their game is connected with their knowledge of trains. It would nevertheless be possible for the children of a tribe unacquainted with trains to learn this game from others, and to play it without knowing that it was copied from anything. One might say that the game did not make the same *sense* to them as to us.)" Cf. *Z*, sec.144 and the sections of *PI* on "point (*Witz*)."

34. Cf. *PO*, p. 447, where Wittgenstein distinguishes the everyday concept of privacy from the metaphysical pseudo-concept "super-privacy." The slave masters are not mentioned in these notes. The idea that they might rationalize their practice in terms of this metaphysical concept is my own.

35. *PO*, p. 133. Just prior to the quoted phrase Wittgenstein remarks that "much too little is made of the fact that we count the words 'soul' and 'spirit' as part of our educated vocabulary."

36. *BB*, p. 65: "I want to play chess, and a man gives the white king a paper crown, leaving the use of the piece unaltered . . . "

superstition? It is a picture at the root of our thinking and is to be respected as such and not treated as a superstition.[37] Is it beyond criticism? If, as in the education I imagined for the slave masters' children, it is used so as to drive a wedge between pain and its expression, then it is abused. And this, of course, *is* subject to criticism.

Postscript

I talked about Wittgenstein's story of the slaves with Professor José Benardete in a Syracuse cafe one afternoon in the summer of 1982. He found it troubling, as I recall, even sinister—an example of a kind of thinking that threatens to undermine enlightenment and ethics. At the time, I did not understand what Wittgenstein was doing, but felt sure it wasn't that. It was only after many years that I clarified my thoughts enough to get them down on paper. Then I remembered our conversation and sent him an earlier version of this chapter. He replied with a paper of his own that contains this reference to Wittgenstein's story:

> In cases where it was obvious to us that the slaves were undergoing the keenest pain, as when they "screamed in agony," the masters would pay no heed. "Here, then," writes [Norman] Malcolm, reporting Wittgenstein's position, "is a difference in 'attitude' that is not a matter of believing . . . different facts." So is it not a fact that sometimes you and I suffer pain . . . ?/ Although the suggestion [the last sentence] cannot possibly be reconciled with *PI*, sec. 246 ("other people very often know when I am in pain"), it indicates to what lengths Wittgenstein was prepared to go in order to distance himself from behaviorism. . . . [He] . . . appears to be pretty much stuck with this dichotomy: behaviorism or non-cognitivism.[38]

In the margin, by the last sentence, José penciled: "Can you refute this, Bill?" I'll try.

Behaviorists would on principle deny that pain is something inner; Wittgenstein would not. His argument is against interpreting "the interiority of pain" to mean "I can't *really* show my pain."[39] That misinterpretation, he suggests, arises from trying to force "showing one's pain" into the model of (for

---

37. Based on *CV*, p. 83.

38. Pp. 279–280, op. cit. in note # 13. Benardete is quoting from Malcolm's review of *PI*.

39. The Cartesian (or "private linguist") will want to qualify "I can't show my pain" with "except to myself." To this, Wittgenstein's reply would be: "I give myself an exhibition of something only *in the same way* as I give one to other people"(RPP-II, sec. 595).

example) "showing one's beetle." (Compare with the way Augustine tried to understand "measuring a length of time" on the model of "measuring a length of ribbon.")

Noncognitivism is more confusing. "Is it not a fact," you ask, "that sometimes you and I suffer pain?" Of course. And (as I understand the story) it would also be a fact that the slaves sometimes suffer pain, that the masters know this, *and* that the masters make a practice of always referring to the suffering of slaves in (as it were) sneer quotes. Is it noncognitivism to say that their practice expresses an immoral attitude rather than a mistaken belief?

Vivisectionists in the seventeenth century rationalized their practices by appeal to Cartesian philosophy. Perhaps the slave masters of Wittgenstein's fiction rationalize their practice by appeal to propaganda given out by Cartesian philosopher-scientists. Converting them would be less like making them believe different things, more like making them *do* different things. We want them to picture the subjugated people differently, and to free them. For this we need not so much to instruct as to exhort.

CHAPTER FOUR

Color and Number

There is in general complete agreement in the judgments of colors made by those who have been diagnosed normal. . . . There is in general no such agreement over the question whether an expression of feeling is genuine or not.

—*Philosophical Investigations*, p. 227

Disputes do not break out (among mathematicians, say) over the question whether a rule has been obeyed or not. . . . That is part of the framework on which the working of our language is based. . . .

—*Philosophical Investigations*, sec. 240

COLOR GRAMMAR

Colors spur us to philosophize. Perhaps that explains Goethe's passion for the theory of colors. (CV, p. 66)

Phenomenological Problems

In the year 1810 Johann Wolfgang von Goethe, a painter and natural philosopher as well as a great poet, published *Zur Farbenlehre*, a book opposing Newtonian color theory. Goethe's work was a major stimulus to Wittgenstein's reflections on the topic.[1]

Newton claimed that white contains all the colors, a claim that struck Goethe as absurd. Whatever Newton's experiments with the prism might show, it could not be *that*. Wittgenstein agreed with Goethe but thought his point could be more clearly expressed as follows:

---

1. Most of these reflections have been collected by editor G.E.M. Anscombe in a volume entitled *Remarks on Color* (RC). Most were composed in the last months of Wittgenstein's life.

> [W]e may call lilac a reddish-whitish-blue or brown a blackish-red-
> dish-yellow—but we *cannot* call a white a yellowish-reddish-
> greenish-blue, or the like. (RC, sec. I-72)

Newton's experiments could not possibly prove that white is a blend of colors
in *that* sense. Similarly, even if mixing red with yellow paints somehow yielded
black paint, we would not call black a blend of red and yellow—an observation instructively developed in the following dialogue between Wittgenstein
and the now-famous A. M. Turing:

> W: [M]ixing paints cannot in a sense show us that orange is red-
> dish yellow. Why shouldn't there be a chemical reaction? . . . So
> we do not use experience as our criterion for orange being a blend
> of red and yellow . . .
> T: In this case, isn't one using "mixture" rather as one uses "multi-
> ply"?
> W: Exactly . . . We are *calculating* with these color terms. The rela-
> tion between: (1) mixing paints actually . . . and (2) saying "red
> and yellow gives orange"—is the same as the relation between: (a)
> "two apples and two apples normally result in four apples," and (b)
> "2 + 2 = 4" (LFM, p. 234)

While (a) is empirical and descriptive, (b) is logical and normative.

Although he used many of the same forms of words as Newton ("mix-
ture of colors," for example), what Goethe was trying to express was more like
a proposition of pure mathematics than of experimental physics. And what he
needed was not a better theory than Newton's, but something entirely different. "A physical theory . . . cannot solve the problems that motivated Goethe,
even if he himself didn't solve them either" (*RC*, sec. III-206). The problems
that motivated Goethe—whether green is a blend of blue and yellow, for
example—could be called "phenomenological problems" (*RC*, sec. I-53).
Sensitive as he was to such problems, Goethe did not clearly grasp their conceptual or logical character, and was therefore unable to solve them.

All meaningful phenomenological problems are (as Wittgenstein sees
them) *logical* problems—and therefore not to be solved by appeal to experience of *any* kind, whether direct ("phenomenological") or indirect ("experimental"). For while the "indirect" appeal could solve no *phenomenological*
problem, the "direct" appeal could solve *no kind* of problem—it would leave us
with one person "seeing" that green's a blend of blue and yellow, and another
"seeing" that it's not.

"A phenomenology" would be something midway between science and
logic.[2] If you believed in a phenomenology of color, you would defend your

---

2. See *RC*, sec. II–3.

claims about the colors by saying, "Just *look* at the colors in nature!" That, however, would be misguided: "For looking does not teach us anything about the concepts of colors" (*RC*, sec. I–72).

> Do not believe that you have the concept of color within you because you look at a colored object—however you look. (Any more than you possess the concept of a negative number by having debts.) (Z, sec. 332)

There is no *phenomenology*, but there are *phenomenological problems*.[3] Phenomenological problems call for the analysis of concepts, but "the method of phenomenology"—looking at colored objects in a certain way ("directly, without presuppositions")—is irrelevant to that. Consider, for example, the problem of whether green is a primary color rather than (as the conventional wisdom would have it) a blend of blue and yellow. Suppose I say I know the answer directly, by looking at the colors:

> [Then] how do I know that I mean the same by the words "primary colors" as some other person who is also inclined to call green a primary color? No,—here language games decide. (*RC*, sec. I-6)

If we call red, yellow, and blue "primary colors," what do we mean? Can we *see* what makes them primary rather than intermediary (mixed, blended) colors? Yes—but not by looking at colored objects. We need to look at our language games with the color words.

In chess, some pieces are knights, others bishops, etc.; learning the chessmen is learning the different ways or "techniques" of moving the different pieces. Think of the color words as "pieces in a language game"; calling a color term "primary" is like calling attention to a particular chessman's technique of use. Now we can rephrase our question about green as whether the technique or way of using "green" in the language game is analogous to the way of using "red," "yellow," and "blue"—rather than to the way of using "orange" and "purple."

---

3. See *RC*, sec. I-53. The negative remark about phenomenology should not be taken as a rejection of everything that has gone under the name. Properly understood, there is such a thing as phenomenology; properly understood, "phenomenology is grammar" (quoted from Wittgenstein's "Big Typescript" by Nicholas Gier, *Wittgenstein and Phenomenology*, p. 437). And my impression is that some thinkers within the phenomenological movement itself—notably Heidegger—would be sympathetic to Wittgenstein's equation. (See the article by Hatab and Brenner, listed in the bibliography.)

The trouble with phenomenology, as Wittgenstein understands it, is that it gives us the wrong directions for disclosing essence. It points to objects rather than to techniques of use:

> One can say: Whoever has a word explained by reference to a patch of color only knows *what* is meant to the extent that he knows *how* the word is to be used. That is to say: there is no grasping or understanding of an object, only the grasping of a technique. (*RPP* II, sec. 296)

Why? Suppose I point to a patch and say: "The people where I come from call that 'boo.'" You will understand me only if you know how to use color words and understand that "boo" is supposed to be such a word. If you learned color talk, you mastered a technique of operating with words which you can now go on to apply to this new word.[4]

The meaning of a word is not like something you might catch hold of with a pair of tweezers.[5] Understanding a meaning is catching on to a use, not catching hold of an object.

Suppose I point to samples of red, blue, and yellow, saying that *these* are what we call "primary colors." Understanding what I mean is not a matter of "abstracting" something they all have in common; it is a matter of knowing how to use them as elements in the language game of blending colors and ordering them into a series.

The solution to the problem whether green is also a primary color is to be found by attending to the activities and practices (the language games) in which techniques of using "color words" are learned and employed. For example, consider a language game involving the word *yellowish* in which things are put in a certain order; through it

> I can learn, in agreement with other people, to recognize yellowish and still more yellowish red, green, brown and white./ In the course of this I learn to proceed independently just as I do in arithmetic. (*RC*, sec. III-110)[6]

Now consider a language game in which one is told to mix a green less yellowish than a given yellowish green, or to pick it out from a set of color samples. A less yellowish green would not be necessarily a *bluer* one. "[A]nd someone may also be given the task of choosing—or mixing—a green that is neither yellowish nor bluish" (*RC*, sec. III-158). Having recalled such language games, we now perceive a reason for calling green a primary rather than an intermediary

---

4. Compare *LFM*, p. 182 (quoted above on p. 35).
5. Compare *RPP* II, sec. 296.
6. On "proceed independently," see *BB*, pp. 93 (# 30) and 104–105 (# 50).

(blended, mixed) color. Orange (taken as a paradigm intermediary color) is "between" red and yellow; consequently, a less yellowish orange is necessarily a redder one, and conversely. But *green* is not like that: a less yellowish green is *not* necessarily a bluer one, nor conversely.

Grammatical Investigations

Recollecting language games is the heart of what Wittgenstein calls "a grammatical investigation." In such an investigation our attention is directed not toward phenomena but toward "the *possibilities* of phenomena" (*PI*, sec. 90). We direct our attention to such "possibilities" by recollecting the kind of statement we make about phenomena. We remember, for example, that "It's bluish green" would count as a statement about the color of wallpaper while "It's yellowish blue" would not.[7]

Grammatical rules exclude certain "moves" and permit others, thereby defining a linguistic practice. They are more like the rules of a game than like empirical "rules," i.e., inductive generalizations. For while inductive generalizations (e.g., that vinegar curdles milk) are (truly or falsely) descriptive, rules of grammar are not. Rules of grammar are no more descriptive than are rules of a game.

The grammar of language differs from rules of a game in the way it informs everyday life—with its practices of describing, commanding, measuring, greeting, thanking, etc.: "The rule-governed nature of our languages permeates our life" (*RC*, sec. III-303). So the rules of grammar are in a sense *not* arbitrary: they are held fast by the human life and practice that surrounds them. So, for example, the rule that orange is a blend of red and yellow is held fast by the kind of employment color words have in our lives. People who could not understand us when we say that orange is a kind of reddish yellow or yellowish red would not be able to analyze blends of color or learn the use of "*x*-ish *y*."[8] This would be a difference in "form of life" rather than a difference in opinion.[9]

When Wittgenstein calls grammar arbitrary, his purpose is to combat a certain philosophical temptation:

> One is tempted to justify rules of grammar by sentences like "But there really are four primary colors." And the saying that the rules of grammar are arbitrary is directed against the possibility of this

---

7. "What makes a string of signs a significant description of (for instance) the color, shape, or number of an object?" This is the defining question of what I want to call *phenomenological grammar*.

8. *RC*, sec. III-129.

9. Cf. *PI*, sec. 241.

> justification, which is constructed on the model of justifying a sentence by pointing to what verifies it. (Z, sec. 331)

Talk of justifying the proposition that there are four dimes in the drawer by pointing to what verifies it makes sense; talk of justifying the proposition that there are four primary colors by pointing to what verifies it does not make sense.

Wittgenstein does sometimes attempt to justify a particular grammatical *remark*. His procedure is to demonstrate that it expresses a rule actually governing our practice with words and helping to make it what it is. A grammatical remark about a word, if true, corresponds to the word's grammar, i.e., to its use in the language. But it means nothing to speak of the grammar itself as true, or to talk of pointing to what makes it true. So if you say that color grammar is made true by "the nature of the colors themselves," we respond with a puzzled "The nature of *what?*" For is it not *grammar* that tells us what kind of object (e.g., color, shape, or sensation) something is?[10] "Justifying color grammar in terms of the nature of color" would be to *justifying* what "the left hand giving the right hand a gift" would be to *giving*.[11]

Essence and Grammar

The essence of color is not expressed by experiments. (Here Wittgenstein agrees with Goethe.) When experimental physics talks about colors, it presupposes grammar. For it builds its theories on descriptions of color phenomena.[12] And whatever determines which descriptions are descriptions of *color* phenomena should be called the essence of color, if anything should.

Recollecting the color grammar we go by in practice and presenting it in a connected, perspicuous way would give us "a picture of the essence" of color. For essence is here expressed by grammar.[13]

But why not say that physics, with its sophisticated language of wave lengths, etc., tells us the *real* nature of color? Physics correlates, for its own purposes, a *new* language game with the ancient and everyday language game of color talk. Although this new game enables us to produce certain predictions and explanations, it is no substitute for the old one. For it is in terms of the old one that the phenomena physics explains are described in the first place. Physics correlates color impressions with hidden physical systems but does not show what the colors *are*; it states propositions *about* the colors but

---

10. Compare *PI*, sec. 373.
11. Compare *PI*, sec. 268.
12. See *PR*, p. 51.
13. Cf. *PI*, sec. 371.

does not elucidate what kind of objects those propositions are about. Nor is it supposed to.

"Reddish Green"?

Wittgenstein is reported to have said the following in a 1930's lecture:

> The color circle is used in psychology to represent the scheme of colors. But it is really a part of grammar, not of psychology. It tells us what we can do: we can speak of a greenish blue but not of a greenish red, etc.[14]

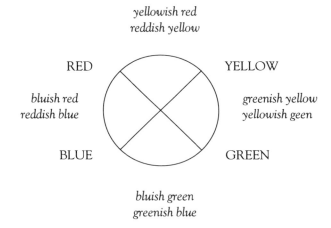

yellowish red
reddish yellow

RED   YELLOW

bluish red   *greenish yellow*
reddish blue   *yellowish geen*

BLUE   GREEN

bluish green
greenish blue

It turns out that grammar is more like geometry than psychology. For example, the grammar that gives no place to "greenish red" on the color circle would be like the geometry that excludes "biangle" from the series of regular plane figures.

> If I had taught someone to use the names of the . . . primary colors, and the suffix "ish" then I could give him orders such as "Paint a greenish white here!"—But now I say to him "Paint a reddish green!" I observe his reaction. Maybe he will mix green and red and not be satisfied with the result; finally he may say "There's no such thing as a reddish green."—Analogously I could have gotten him to tell me [admit]: "There's no such thing as a regular biangle!" (*RPP* II, sec. 422)

---

14. *WLL*, p. 8 (text modified: "circle" substituted for "octahedron"). Compare the color circle with the paradigms and other devices employed by language teachers. The point of such devices is to provide "perspicuous representations" of grammar. They are not presented as *interpretations* of the grammar.

Just as we do not continue the *angle series*,

        quadrangle (☐)
        triangle   (△)

with

        biangle (— ??),

so we do not continue the *ish* series,

        reddish blue   (certain grapes)
        reddish yellow (certain oranges),

with

        reddish green (a dead leaf??).

And *that* we do not thus continue is part of what determines the concepts "constructing a figure" and "mixing a color."

If someone were to speak of "reddish greens" or "regular biangles," we should not disagree with him—at least not in the way in which we would disagree with someone who spoke of nonaddictive heroin or nonfattening butter. We should say, perhaps, that he was talking of something logically, not just physically impossible. But what does saying "logically impossible" amount to? Consider the word formation *reddish green*. It is not that we see it means something impossible. Rather, we refuse to give it a meaning, a use in language. Why? Because to do so would upset our language game. The sentence "*x* is reddish green" is a word formation arrived at by continuing a certain line of the practice of using sentences. And if we gave it a use, we would feel that we had broken the line of our ordinary practice of language.[15] And it is the existence of such lines of practice that gives words meaning and makes them language.

Consider "reddish green" again. It is not that we first grasp the meanings of the words, analyze them, and then deduce that nothing could be reddish green; it is that the meaning of the color words is *constituted* by the fact that we regularly exclude some word formations (e.g., "reddish green") from the language and permit others (e.g., "reddish yellow").

People who called the color brown (for instance) "reddish green" would be either misusing language (perhaps playfully) or possessed of concepts other than ours. And if they really had different concepts, this would have to be shown in our inability to figure out their use of words.[16] And if we couldn't quite figure out their use of words, we would hesitate to call them *color* words. Thus:

> [E]ven if there were also people for whom it was natural to use the expressions "reddish green" or "yellowish blue" in a consistent manner and who perhaps also exhibit abilities which we lack, we

---

15. See lecture 24 in *LFM*.
16. See *RC*, sec. II-123.

would still not be forced to recognize that they see *colors* which we do not see. There is, after all, no *commonly* accepted criterion for what is a color, unless it is one of our colors. (*RC*, sec. I-14)

Suppose we find people who claim to differentiate between the colors of two chemical compounds that to us look exactly the same. If they call the one "brown" and the other "reddish green," we might want to say they know of a color that we do not—but then again, we might not.[17] Compare with the case of someone's claiming to have "trisected an angle with compass and ruler": although he does something that looks like bisecting and that always yields three equal angles as measured with a protractor, geometricians will deny that what he does is relevantly analogous to what they call "bisection."[18]

There is a sense in which we cannot conceive of "an alternative color grammar," that is, of color concepts different from our own. For:

> [I]sn't it precisely the geometry [grammar] of colors that shows us what we're talking about, i.e. that we are talking about colors?/ "The colors" are not things that have definite properties, so that one could straight off look for or imagine colors that we don't yet know, *or* imagine someone who knows different ones than we do. It is quite possible that, under certain circumstances, we would say that people know colors that we don't know, but we are not forced to say this, for there is no indication as to what we should regard as adequate analogies to our colors, in order to be able to say it. (*RC*, secs. III-86, 127)

Compare colors with apples. Since apples *are* things that have definite properties, we can conceive an alternative pomology as we cannot an alternative color grammar.[19] "Discovering a new color" would be analogous, not to "discovering a new species of apple" but to "discovering a new kind of number." For "kinds of number can only be distinguished by the arithmetical rules relating to them" (*PR*, p. 130). Colors are like numbers and geometrical figures, and unlike apples and chemical elements, in that it is *grammar* rather than experience that tells us how many kinds there are.[20]

---

17. Cf. *RC*, sec III-163.

18. Cf. *PI*, sec. 237.

19. In the terminology of the *Tractatus*, "apple" and "slab" are concepts proper while "color" and "number" are formal concepts.

20. Although Riemann invented a grammar that was found to be more convenient for some purposes than Euclid's, it would be misleading to say he discovered new facts about space and parallel lines. Riemann discovered (or invented) not facts but concepts—concepts related to ordinary ones in such a way that mathematicians agreed to call them "geometrical." Although they had good reason for thus extending the use of "geometrical concept," they could have called it a misuse. (See *RC*, sec. III-127.)

"Transparent White"?

"A perspicuous representation produces just that understanding which consists in 'seeing connections'" (*PI*, sec. 122). I conclude by attempting a perspicuous representation of some remarks by Wittgenstein on the use of color words.

Green is not a blend of yellow and blue. Someone who denies this should reflect on the difference between green and orange. Even though green can in fact be produced by mixing blue and yellow paints or lights, it is not akin to blue and yellow in the way orange (for instance) is akin to red and yellow.[21] For while it makes sense to call orange a reddish yellow, it is senseless to call green a bluish yellow.[22]

White is not a blend of colors. White is an *element* in blends of color, along with black and the primary colors.

White and black are excluded from the color circle. Though counted as colors in some contexts (as when naming the color of flags or glass beads), white and black have no place in the color circle. For not only do they mix with all the colors; they also mix with their opposite pole.[23] The "opposite poles" of the color circle, red-green and yellow-blue, do not mix. So there are no blends of red and green, or of yellow and blue, in the way there are blends of white and black ("the shades of grey").

White is not a transparent color. Once we learn to go to the store to buy paper of various colors, we can be taught to do likewise for transparent plastic sheets. And once we learn a new technique or two (holding the sheets up to daylight, looking through them at something white), we are able to obey orders to buy transparencies of a color we were never asked to buy before. We have learned how to proceed independently.

Everyone will know how to obey an order to buy some transparent orange plastic film. But many will react with puzzlement if asked to buy transparent *white* film. ("What do you mean?," "Are you setting a riddle?," "Do you want us to buy some of that cloudy polyethylene film used for very cheap storm windows?") Here we do not know how to proceed independently.

To continue the series "transparent yellow, transparent orange, transparent . . . " with *white* provokes the reaction: "That's not going on in the same way!" In order to understand this reaction, we need to see how it is connected with the rules of our practice with color terms.

---

21. Compare *RC*, sec. III-113.

22. I discussed this in more detail earlier in this essay. See also Mounce's review of *RC* in *Philosophical Quarterly* 30 (1980), pp. 159–160—a piece to which my understanding of Wittgenstein on color is indebted.

23. Compare *RC*, sec. III-85.

Consider the rule that something white placed behind a colored and fully transparent medium appears in the color of that medium. This rule for the spatial interpretation of visual experience could be formulated as a rule for painters:

> "If you want to portray something white behind something that is transparent and red, you have to paint it red." If you paint it white, it doesn't look as though it is behind the red thing. (*RC*, sec. III-173)

Now if we attempt to apply this rule to "a white transparent medium," we are led to say that anything white placed behind such a medium would have to *look* white. But then it could not be a fully transparent medium. For a surface that looked white-on-white would give no impression of depth, no impression of something white *behind* it. (Looking out a window gives the impression of depth. But standard window glass is colorless, not white.)

Although it does not function as the name of a transparent color, "white" does figure in descriptions of the appearance of transparent media. For example: "The plastic sheet has whitened and therefore lost some of its transparency"; "That green transparent glass looks white in the glare of sunlight"; "Notice the white highlights on the surface of the glass."

Discussing "metallic and luminous" as well as "transparent and opaque" colors, Wittgenstein demonstrates that "the logic of the concept is just much more complicated than it might seem" (*RC*, sec. III-106). These remarks on color are the final expression of a career-long investigation of our "life world"[24] in all its variety and richness. ("There are just many more language games than are dreamt of in the philosophy of Carnap and others" [*RPP* I, sec. 920].)[25]

ARITHMETIC AS GRAMMAR

> There is no religious denomination in which the misuse of metaphysical expressions has been responsible for so much sin as it has in mathematics. (*CV*, p. 1)

Numbers

Philosophy of mathematics may have commenced with the wonder evoked in Pythagoras at numbers and their properties. Certainly the Pythagoreans

---

24. Associated with phenomenology, this concept was also at work in *TLP* (see 5.621). Compare "forms of life" in *PI*.

25. I defend Wittgenstein's approach to color against the criticisms of two leading "color philosophers," Jonathan Westphal and C.L. Hardin, in "'Brownish Yellow' and 'Reddish Green.'"

passed this wonder along to later generations, where it found expression in a question, "What is a number?," and in a series of answers:

> Numbers are signs on paper (nominalism)
> . . . ideas in the mind (conceptualism)
> . . . eternal, immutable objects (metaphysical,
> "platonic" realism).

Wittgenstein shared the Pythagorean wonder but added to it another of his own: wonder—amazement—at the questions and answers the Pythagorean wonder had provoked. Wittgenstein's wonder might be expressed in the question, "Why do philosophers ask, 'What is a *number*?'—but never 'What is a *chair*?' ":

> "What is a chair?," by comparison with "What is 3?" seems simple.
> For if one is asked what a chair is, one can point to something or
> give some sort of description; but if asked what the number 3 is,
> one is at a loss.[26]

On finding nothing to point to but the mark, the numeral "3," we are at first tempted to say with the nominalist that 3 just *is* the mark. But then we wonder whether this leaves out the important thing, the *meaning* of the mark. For if a mathematical proposition were just a complex of marks, then it would be "dead and utterly uninteresting, whereas it obviously has a kind of life" (*BB*, p. 4). What then must be added to give it life?

> On seeing that defining the number 3 as the sign won't do, we tend
> to say that since it is not the sign it is something else. (p. 152)

This "something else" would be what the sign *means*, and what it means must be of an entirely different order from any sign, something in a different category of being. It occurs to us now that a sign is a manifest, material object, and that no such object could possibly give the life of meaning to a sign. And now comes the thought: this mysterious life-giving thing would have to be of an un-manifest, mental nature. This is the "conceptualism" mentioned earlier, the view that numbers exist only in the mind, as objects of mental awareness or "ideas."

Saying that the meaning of a sign is an idea suggests that it (the meaning) exists only for my mind or yours. But in that case there would be no science of numbers—no arithmetic: there would just be a psychology of your

---

26. *WLA*, p. 151. Unless otherwise indicated, page references will be to that book (the Ambrose/Macdonald notes on Wittgenstein's 1932–35 lectures).

"number ideas" and mine. There would be no common object of knowledge and therefore no science.

Shall we say, then, that numbers are *neither* material, like signs, *nor* mental, like ideas—but of a different order entirely? But then how are we to conceive this "different order"? If numbers belong not to a material or mental realm but to a Fregean (or platonic) "third realm,"[27] then how are they supposed to relate to the objects we count and measure every day?

Nominalism, conceptualism, metaphysical realism: each has its own problem. And we suspect that a fourth philosophy of mathematics would have its own problem too. So let us try a different tack. Let us go back to the beginning and recall that the inquiry got started with "What is a number?" What led the Pythagoreans, what leads *us* to ask this question? What is in back of it? According to Wittgenstein, the question

> "What is 3?" arises from a jumble of misunderstandings, one of which is due to our having the word "meaning" in our language. "Meaning" is thought to stand for (1) something to which one can point, or (2) something in the mind. Suppose I ask whether the word "7" is meaningless in the sentence "There are 7 men in the room." Although it does not stand for something which can be pointed to, everyone would reply that it is not meaningless, it is not superfluous. It has a function in the sentence. It is not the same as clearing-the-throat sounds. Although "function of a word" is not a definition of "meaning of a word," it is always useful to replace "meaning" by "function." (p. 151)

Wittgenstein's advice to philosophers of mathematics is to replace questions such as "What is the number three?" with questions such as "How do 'three' and related words function in our language?"

> Don't ask for a definition; get clear about the grammar. By getting clear about the use of the word "number" we cease to ask the question "What is number?" (p. 164)

Nominalists in answering that question appear to imply that *the number 3* and *the sign "3"* may replace each other. We see that this is wrong when we see that the italicized expressions are not used in the same way. For "we can say that the sign '3' is red or written crookedly, but not that the number 3 is" (p. 151). Conceptualists and platonists saw this difference in use and rightly urged it against the nominalist; they went wrong only when they proceeded to con-

---

27. On Frege's "third realm," see "The Thought: A Logical Inquiry." On the kind of importance the idea of such a realm can still have in a Wittgensteinian philosophy of mathematics, see Diamond's *Realistic Spirit*, "The Face of Necessity." (And compare its place in mathematics with that of "the picture of the inner" in psychology.)

clude that a difference in use must be correlated with something else, "its meaning." To these philosophers Wittgenstein's advice is to think of the meaning *as* the use, rather than as something "correlated with" or "behind" the use.

Rules

Language is rule-governed. To understand a language is to understand the rules governing the meaningful use of the words and other signs belonging to it.

Compare language to an old European city, such as Vienna. Mathematics is a part of it, with differential calculus (for example) in a newer suburban area and arithmetic in the old city center. The philosophical problem "What is a number?" expresses the disorientation we sometimes experience when strolling through the center of our language, a disorientation best overcome by recollecting rules for the use of the number words. For example, we may need to recollect that

> "3" has different uses in the sentences "There are 3 men here" and "2 + 1 = 3". . . . The arithmetic sentence in which "3" occurs is a rule about the use of the word "3." The relation of this sentence to a sentence such as "There are 3 men here" is that between rule of grammar about the word "3" and a sentence in which the word "3" is used. The application of a mathematical sentence occurring in our language is not to show us what is true or false, but what is sense and what is nonsense . . . (p. 152)/ The statement that I had two apples, that Johnson gave me two more, and that I ate the four apples, is in accordance with the rule [2 + 2 = 4]. It makes sense; whereas in the light of the rule "4 − 5 ≠ 1," I had four apples of which I gave away five and had one left, does not make sense. (pp. 155–156)

Arithmetical propositions express rules for the use of numerals. What, then, are rules?

> It is misleading to say that a rule is a statement, a statement about a mark, for then there is a temptation to say it states that we in our society use a sign in such and such a way. (p. 153)

To say that arithmetical equations are rules, and that rules are statements about how certain signs are used in a given society is misleading, inasmuch as "rules play a different role than statements" (p. 153). "All Englishmen use these signs in this way": *this* is a statement about the use of signs. When we hear such a statement, our first thought is to ask whether it is true or not. It is misleading to think of a rule as such a statement because that blurs the distinction between arithmetic and its application. The statement "If A gives me 2 apples and *B* gives me 2 apples, then I have 4 apples in all" is an application of the rule that 2 + 2 = 4. The statement is true or false, the rule is not.[28]

But, again, what is a rule? So far we have been told only what it is not.

> A rule [Wittgenstein suggests] is best described as being like a garden path in which you are trained to walk, and which is convenient. You are taught arithmetic by a process of training, and this becomes one of the paths in which you walk. You are not compelled to do so, but you just do it. (p. 155)

Children often set up rules for themselves "just for the fun of it," then (as it were) allow the rules to compel them. But they also receive rigorous training from their elders, notably in arithmetic. Not set up "just for the fun of it," arithmetical rules are learned in and through training in the practices of counting and measuring.

Arithmetical rules are not simply stipulated. They can be derived from other rules within a system of rules. When we learned arithmetic we learned the techniques and practices governed by this system. We learned it as the first stage in a process of acculturation that leads eventually to "full citizenship in the community of mathematicians."[29]

"2 + 2 = 4" (for example) is a *useful* rule: "*most* useful—we couldn't do without it for a thousand reasons, not just *one*" (*LFM*, p. 249). And so arithmetic is not a game. Its rules have applications in our life in a way rules of a game do not.

(Wittgenstein characterizes his task in philosophy of mathematics as follows:

> What I have to do is something like describing the office of a king; —in doing which I must never fall into the error of explaining the kingly dignity by the king's usefulness, but I must leave neither his usefulness nor his dignity out of account. [*RFM*, p. 357]

So his remarks on the usefulness of mathematical rules are not to be read as a prelude to a "pragmatic reduction" of the subject.[30])

Experience

Are the rules of arithmetic conclusions from experience?

---

28. Based on *LFM*, p. 154.

29. The preceding paragraph is based on *RFM*, pp. 228, 243, and 429.

30. Nor does he understand "usefulness" in a narrowly utilitarian way. See *RFM*, pp. 126–127: "The motto here is always: Take a *wider* look round."

> [I]f whenever we counted 2 and 3 and the result was 4, we might
> say our rule must change. Or we might say that one of the beads
> had vanished, i.e., we might never alter the calculation $2 + 3 = 5$,
> though it might be very inconvenient not to. When we say $2 + 3$
> *must* be 5, this shows that we have determined what is to count as
> correct; the *must* is a sign of a calculation. . . . / If we report that in
> counting with normal chalk, $2 + 3$ always equals 5, but with Dover
> chalk 8, it is clear that we are talking of an experiment. . . . But we
> could have started with either as a standard for judging experi-
> ments. . . . The facts do not compel us to accept one of them, but
> suggest the one we adopt. (p. 160)

Although few experimental results are ever adopted in practice as standards or
rules for judging future experiments, in theory any experimental result might
be so adopted:

> Every empirical proposition may serve as a rule if it is fixed, like a
> machine part, made immovable, so that now the whole represen-
> tation turns around it and becomes part of the coordinate system,
> independent of facts. (*RFM*, p. 437)

"As an optical instrument makes light come from various sources in a particular way to form a pattern," so this "coordinate system" will (if functional)
guide empirical research and organize experimental results.[31]

We may, therefore, be persuaded to adopt one rule rather than another
by experience, when experiment shows it to be the more convenient way. But
we may also be persuaded to do it by experience in a different sense, "the experience of a new aspect." For example:

> What does one discover when one discovers . . . that two right
> isosceles triangles put together give a rectangle? A new experience
> is involved, an experience of *a new aspect*. We say "Oh, that has
> never struck me; but now I see it must be so." We do not say this in
> the case of a genuine experiment. (pp. 179–180)

Suppose we had never seen a pentagram inscribed in a pentagon and
now we do.

---

31. *RFM*, p. 241. The broadly Kantian insight of this and the previous quotation from
the *Remarks* was to become a major theme of Wittgenstein's *On Certainty*.

Does the new experience teach us a timeless mathematical truth? No. For, although "The pentagram fits the pentagon" seems to be proved by experience, its *use* is entirely different from that of propositions proved by experience.

"My hand has five fingers" functions as an empirical proposition or statement of fact. "The pentagram has five outer vertices" functions as a geometrical proposition or rule of language. Although the two sentences look or sound very much alike, their depth grammar differs enormously.[32] Consider, for example, the propositions "My hand fits the pentagon" and "The pentagram fits the pentagon." Although they sound alike, they have entirely different uses: the first states a *result* of a one-to-one correlation, the second formulates a *rule* of one-to-one correlation.

Internal Properties

Philosophy of mathematics is a logical investigation. From what does such an investigation take its rise? "It takes its rise, not from an interest in the facts of nature, nor from a need to grasp causal connections: but from an urge to understand the basis, or essence, of everything empirical" (*PI*, sec. 89).

What belongs to the essence is "the mark of a concept," not the property of an object.[33] For example, what belongs to the essence of

is a mark of the concepts black and white, not a property of the objects (the patches).

> Whence [then] comes the feeling that "white is lighter than black" expresses something about the *essence* of the two colors? . . . Is it not like this: the picture of a black and white patch serves us *simultaneously* as a paradigm of what we understand by "lighter" and "darker" and as a paradigm for "white" and for "black." (*RFM*, pp. 75-76)

Compare "There are 2 pairs in 4." The feeling that this expresses something about the essence of the numbers comes from such facts as that the figure "| | | |" serves us simultaneously as a paradigm of what we understand by "two two's" and by "four." ("I deposit what belongs to the essence among the paradigms of language" [*RFM*, p. 50].)

It makes sense to say that there was or will be two pairs of socks in a drawer, not that there *was* or *will be* two twos in every four. Propositions about

---

32. See *WLA*, p. 172, and (on "depth grammar"), *PI*, sec. 664.
33. Based on *RFM*, p. 64.

essence are timeless or tenseless, propositions about objects are not; arithmetical propositions are about essence, empirical propositions are not.

Contrast calculation with experiment. "We regard the calculation as demonstrating an *internal property* (a property of the *essence*) of the structures" (*RFM*, p. 73). That two quarts of water mixed with two quarts of vodka give four quarts of liquid states (if true) an "external," empirical property; that two twos make four states an "internal," logical property.

Rational Persuasion

Wittgenstein stresses the importance of "perspicuous representation" in mathematics (as well as in philosophical investigation and aesthetics). A representation or picture is "perspicuous" when it helps us to gain a clear view of some domain, so that we can "see connections" (*PI*, sec. 122). For example, the following representation of "5 × 4 = 4 × 5" persuades us to accept the commutativity rule for multiplication (m × n = n × m):

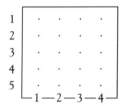

It functions as the kind of rational persuasion called "proof." "The 'proved proposition' [m × n = n × m] expresses what is to be read off from the proof picture" (*RFM*, p. 161).

Wittgenstein gave a course in philosophy of mathematics at Cambridge in 1939. One of his colleagues, John Wisdom, attended the classes and once told of a dispute he had as a boy with his mathematics tutor; Wittgenstein used this story in his discussion of proof:

> A mathematical proof persuades us by making certain connections. It puts this (126 × 631 = ___) in the middle of a huge system—it gives it a place. We are taught to adopt any rule that can be produced in such a way. . . . / [W]hat the proof does is to make the connection: by this connection it may or may *not* persuade you. . . . We may have a particular prejudice against these numbers. . . . / Consider Wisdom's case. . . . The master had said that 3 × 0 = 0 and Wisdom had said that 3 × 0 = 3. What would be said by each side to prove his case?/ Well, Wisdom says that if three cows are multiplied by 0 then that means they have not multiplied at all, and so there are still three cows. The master might then say, "Look: 3 × 2 = 3 + 3; 3 × 1 = 3; and so 3 × 0 = 0." He

makes Wisdom surprised at having to admit that 3×1 is not equal
to 3×0. (LFM, pp. 134-135)

In other words: Wisdom said that $3 \times 0 = 3$; he reasoned that to say (for
example) that three cows have been multiplied by zero would mean that they
have not been multiplied at all and are still three. His teacher used the following analogy to get him to change his mind:

> Three multiplied by three = three threes ($3 \times 3 = 3 + 3 + 3$),
> Three multiplied by two = two threes ($3 \times 2 = 3 + 3$),
> Three multiplied by one = one three ($3 \times 1 = 3$),
> Therefore, by analogy,
> Three multiplied by zero = zero threes ($3 \times 0 = 0$).

Wisdom, from the beginning, accepted the premises of the argument.
Through the "perspicuous representation" of these premises supplied by his
tutor, he came to agree that 3×0 is equal neither to 3×1, nor to 3.

Suppose Wisdom had objected to one of the steps in the teacher's argument, or doubted the force of the analogy? Any child being taught mathematics may in the end have to be told, "This is how it's done! 'Explanations come
to an end somewhere' (PI, sec. 1)."

Suppose the child resisted "the way it's done" and persisted in going his
own, different way. We might say that such a child is unteachable when it
comes to arithmetic.

Compare mathematical with religious instruction. A child being taught
how to pray may in the end be told, "This is how it's done." If he persists in
doing it "in his own way," we might conclude that he cannot be taught our
religion. We wondered, in the mathematical case, if the pupil would ever *learn*
arithmetic—not whether he would learn *our* arithmetic.

Calculation and other arithmetical activities depend on a wide measure
of agreement in order to get going at all; praying and other religious activities
do not. And so the terms *religion* and *prayer* encompass a far greater diversity
than do *arithmetic* and *calculation*. It is clear that bizarre unorthodox beliefs
(such as "God commands us to hate strangers") may still be religious beliefs; it
is not clear that bizarre beliefs (such as "$3 \times 0 = 3$") may still be *mathematical*
beliefs.[34]

Instruction in religion is typically a matter of teaching an orthodoxy or
set of authoritatively approved beliefs and practices. Arguments deployed to
defend the orthodoxy are notoriously inconclusive. It is not just that they may

---

34. I relied in this paragraph less on Wittgenstein than on Gareth Moore, *Believing in
God*, pp. 32–33. (Wittgenstein discusses the notion of "alternative arithmetics" in
RFM-I, secs. 142–152.)

persuade *me* but not *you*; it is also that one's acceptance or rejection of such arguments is not normally counted for or against one's rationality—as it often is in other areas of thought, including arithmetic. ("The reasonable man does *not have* certain doubts" [OC, sec. 220].)

There *is* such a thing as rational persuasion in religion, as distinguished from brainwashing and sophistry. But while religious people demand (or ought to demand) some sort of rational persuasion from their theologians, few if any demand *proofs*—as they do of their mathematicians. Why this is so has something to do with what religion *is*, as contrasted with mathematics. Mathematics (at least on Wittgenstein's account) is basically a motley of techniques for counting and measuring; religion is basically a certain spirit that pervades (or is meant to pervade) everything we do.[35] Mathematics addresses us impersonally, telling us something of what "the reasonable person" believes; religion addresses us personally, telling us of a way of living and assessing life that may be very different from "the reasonable man's."

Religion is not a science. Why then compare it with mathematics? I compare religion with mathematics because of important but often-overlooked respects in which it resembles mathematics more than any empirical science. Its "rational persuasions" are more like proofs in arithmetic or geometry than proofs in engineering or physics.

"The mathematician is not a discoverer; he is an inventor" (*RFM*, p. 111). But may we not *also* say that people discover mathematical truths—as they discover new ways of speaking, new comparisons, new ways of looking at things? The important point is that this "discovery" is not to be compared to what a natural scientist does when she discovers a causal connection or a new star: it is more like what an artist does when he creates a new way of painting, a new meter, or a new kind of song.[36]

Shall we say that people invent religious truths? Not if it is our own religious beliefs we are talking about. For to say that *we* made the religious truths we live by would bespeak an impiety and pride very much at odds with the religious spirit.[37] Here we might follow the suggestion of Plato's *Ion* and say that it is by something other than either discovery or invention that we come by our "saving truths," namely *divine inspiration*. For did the prophets of our religion take any more credit for their prophesies than did the poets of the *Ion* for their poems?

---

35. Compare p. 11, above.

36. Cf. *PI*, sec. 401.

37. Compare the "trademark argument" in Descartes' Third Meditation and Simone Weil's "experimental ontological proof" in *Gravity and Grace*, p. 90.

"Correspondence to Reality"

Mathematics, we want to say, is responsible to reality. And by this we may mean something like:

> "Mathematical propositions don't correspond to *moods*; you can't say one thing now and one thing then." . . . [Or we may mean] "Please don't think of mathematics as something vague which goes on in the mind." (LFM, p. 240)

What, then, *is* the correspondence of mathematical propositions to reality? A main source of confusion here is trying to understand this on the model of the correspondence of a true empirical proposition with fact—whereas it is more like the way a word might be said to correspond to reality. Asked what reality corresponds to the word *chair*, we would all point to much the same things. But what shall we do if asked to point to the reality corresponding to the words *two* or *plus*? Wittgenstein's suggestion is that we point to their *use*.[38] Mathematical words and equations belong to the resources of our language. Whether they are conformable to reality is a matter of whether nature (including *our* nature) makes them resources we need or want to use.

Mathematics is non-arbitrary only in the sense that it has an application. But (to paraphrase *PI*, sec. 520) not everything that *looks* like a mathematical proposition is something we know how to do something with; and when we are tempted to count some quite useless thing as mathematics, that is because we have not considered its application sufficiently. And if we consider the propositions and techniques of certain branches of mathematics sufficiently, we may come to regard some of their "applications" as distinctly fishy.

Wittgenstein argues that much of the charm of transfinite arithmetic comes from seeing it as applying to a transcendent realm of exotic mathematical entities.[39] We might say that his arguments express a kind of *realism* in philosophy of mathematics: a realism determined to steer away from the "fanciful" or "fishy" accounts of the correspondence between mathematics and reality found in metaphysical realism.

---

38. See *LFM*, p. 249. Compare Cora Diamond's "Wittgenstein, Mathematics and Ethics" (to which I am much indebted).

39. See *LFM*, p. 150. Wittgenstein thinks there is a muddle in back of the debate over whether arithmetic is "about a mathematical realm." He means, not that certain mathematical propositions are wrong, but that we think their interest lies in something it does not: "I am *not* saying transfinite propositions are *false*, but that the wrong pictures go with them" (*LFM*, p. 141). For more on these matters, see the "number, transfinite" references in the index of *LFM*.

Can we make sense of *religion*, and of questions about the correspondence of its propositions with reality, without resorting either to metaphysical realism or to an empirical reduction of its concepts? I think this question is behind many of Wittgenstein's remarks on religions and their "grammar"—which are the main subjects of the next chapter.

CHAPTER FIVE

God

I would like to say "This book is written to the glory of God," but nowadays . . . that would not be rightly understood.
—*Philosophical Remarks*, p. 7

How words are understood is not told by words alone. (Theology.)
—*Zettel*, sec. 144

THEOLOGY AS GRAMMAR

Grammar tells us what kind of object anything is. (Theology as grammar.) —*PI*, sec. 373

Grammar

Theology is commonly viewed as speculation about a mysterious Something or Someone. Wittgenstein recommends a different perspective (one he attributes to Luther): "[T]heology is the grammar of the word 'God'" (*WLA*, p. 32). This perspective highlights the fact that many of us first learned a theology in the course of learning the practices of a religion, much as all of us first learned a language in the course of learning how to speak. In learning our native language we learned to use words in the context of various activities: "feet and inches" in connection with measuring lengths, for example. Having learned to measure, we could then acquire knowledge of the length of sticks, ribbons, etc. In learning religious language for the first time, we learned the use of new words in the context of new activities: for example, "God and creation" in connection with the praising, thanking, and asking of prayer. Having mastered this, we were then enabled to participate in a kind of "practice of the presence of God." Calling theology *grammar* is a way of distinguishing it from the sometimes inarticulate "spiritual wisdom" often said to be the fruit of such a practice, such a life.

But—"theology as grammar" (*PI*, sec. 373): doesn't this comparison trivialize theology? Not if we understand that the grammar in question is for teaching and celebrating a new form of life. Appropriated as a mere "form of words," a theology will be forgotten, or transformed into something else— often a vain, hypocritical cover for some purely secular (e.g., hedonistic) life.

"Theology is the grammar of the word 'God'" (*WLA*, p. 32). But didn't Wittgenstein disavow theses in philosophy? Yes—for example in *PI*, secs. 126 and 128; nor is he going against that here. He is recommending (presumably from his own experience) a way of relieving "mental cramp":

> The questions "What is length?," "What is meaning?," "What is the number one?," etc. produce in us a mental cramp. We feel that we can't point to anything in reply to them and yet ought to point to something. (*BB*, p. 1)

If you feel stymied and perplexed by trying to answer the question "What is the number one?," you may find it liberating and illuminating to substitute questions about the use of the numeral "1." Similarly: if (like Wittgenstein) you feel stymied and perplexed by "What is God?," you may find it helpful to substitute questions about the use of the word "God."

"*The* use of the word 'God'?" Aren't the rules for its use modified as we move from one religion to another—from the Greek Olympian religion to Judaism, for example; or from fundamentalist to Anglican Christianity?" It seems clear that they are—sometimes radically. Wittgenstein would acknowledge that diversity and add some such disclaimer as: when I describe a religious language game, I am not trying to insinuate a theory about "the underlying essence of religion"; I am presenting my description as an *object of comparison* meant to throw light on differences as well as similarities in the use of "God" and related words:

> For we can avoid ineptness or emptiness in our assertions only by presenting the model [language game] as what it is, an object of comparison—as, so to speak, a measuring rod; not as a precon-ceived idea to which reality *must* correspond. (The dogmatism into which we fall so easily in doing philosophy.) (*PI*, sec. 131)

God and Judgment Day

Recalling the religious instruction of his childhood,[1] Wittgenstein remarks that the word *God* is radically different in its use or method of func-tioning from other nouns it superficially resembles:

---

1. Joachim Schulte tells us that Wittgenstein's best *Matura* (roughly, college entrance exam) grade was a "superior" in Roman Catholic doctrine. See *Wittgenstein: Eine Einfürung*, p. 9.

> The word "God" is amongst the earliest learnt—pictures and cate-
> chisms, etc. But not the same consequences as with pictures of
> aunts. I wasn't shown that which the picture pictured.[2]

There is no such thing as pointing to what the picture of God pictures. If I am
given a picture of an aunt I've never met, I can use it to identify her when I go
to meet her at the airport. The picture of God has no analogous use.

> ["God"] is used like a word representing a person. God sees,
> rewards, etc./ "Being shown all these things, did you understand
> what this word meant?" I'd say: "Yes and no. I did learn what it
> didn't mean. . . . "

I learned that "God sees me" does not have the same implications as "Aunt
Martha sees me"; learned that one does not speak of God's help as the result of
identifying one helper among others; etc.

> If the question arises as to the existence of a god or God, it plays an
> entirely different role to that of the existence of any person or
> object I ever heard of.

That certain people love me is a matter of experience; that God loves me
is a matter of dogma (biblical texts, etc.). "The love of God" and other
dogmas were part of my training in a particular way of life. These dogmas
permeate prayer, worship, and other activities distinctive to this way of
life. I was praised for participating in them, blamed for neglecting them or
replacing them by "ungodly" practices. What burning the flag is to the
political community, saying there is no God is to the religious community.

> Also, there is this extraordinary use of the word "believe." . . . You
> might say (in the normal use): "You only believe—oh well. . . . "
> Here it is used entirely differently; on the other hand it is not used
> as we generally use the word "know."

In the ordinary use, belief is an inferior cognitive state: to know that a proposition is true is much more desirable than "just believing" it. Is there any such
contrast in normal religious speech?

> If I even vaguely remember what I was taught about God, I might
> say: "Whatever believing in God may be, it can't be believing
> something we can test or find a means of testing."

---

2. This, and all subsequent quotations until further notice, are from "Lectures on
Religious Belief" (in *LC*, students notes edited by Cyril Barrett). *I have rearranged some
of the passages.*

Belief in God is not confidence in an hypothesis. "Is there a God?" is not a question of what we might find as the result of an investigation.[3]

Confidence in a weather forecast is reasonable or unreasonable, depending on whether it is based on sufficient evidence; belief in a Judgment Day is not confidence in a forecast and is neither reasonable nor unreasonable.

> Suppose someone dreamt of the Last Judgment, and said he now knew what it would be like. Suppose someone said: "This is poor evidence." I would say: "If you want to compare it with the evidence for it's raining tomorrow it is no evidence at all." . . . [If it is argued:] "Well, I had this dream . . . therefore . . . Last Judgment," you might say: "For a blunder, that's too big."

Not every false statement is a blunder. If you suddenly wrote down "2 + 21 = 13," we would wonder *what* you were doing, not whether you were making a *mistake* in what you were doing. (One day I saw "26 + 6 = 1" on a bumper sticker. This was no mistake in addition! The map of united Ireland [with 26 southern and 6 northern counties] showed what it was.)

> Here we have people who . . . base enormous things on this evidence. Am I to say they are unreasonable? . . . "Unreasonable" implies, with everyone, rebuke. I want to say: they don't treat this as a matter of reasonability. . . . Not only is it not reasonable, but it doesn't pretend to be. . . . / Why shouldn't one form of life culminate in an utterance of belief in a Last Judgment?/ . . . [This belief] will show, not by reasoning or by appeal to ordinary grounds for belief, but rather by regulating for [everything] in all his life.[4]

"How will this look on Judgment Day?" will always be at the back of this believer's mind. He will see everyday successes and failures in perspective— "the perspective of Eternity."

> It strikes me that a religious belief could only be something like a passionate commitment to a system of reference. Hence, although it's a *belief*, it's really a way of living, or a way of assessing life. . . . (CV, p. 64)

---

3. Some religious teachers certainly do seem to present the existence of God as a (well-supported) scientific hypothesis. If this accurately reflects the central use of the word "God" in their denomination, then they are teaching quite a different religion from the one Wittgenstein learned.

4. Wittgenstein's refusal to treat religious beliefs as hypotheses based (or failing to be based) on evidence does not mean he divorces religion from critical reason. I think of the many remarks in CV in which he subjects the belief in predestination to critical scrutiny. (His initial impression is that it is "ugly nonsense" [p. 32].) I would add that rational persuasion, as opposed to bare assertion and diatribe, has had an important

God and Judgment Day are basic in a certain way of living and assessing life. We are persuaded of their reality if and when the life to which they are basic comes alive for us—perhaps through a spiritual biography, perhaps through experiences of our own.

> Life can educate one to a belief in God. And *experiences* too are what bring this about; but I don't mean visions and other forms of sense experience which show us the "existence of this being," but, e.g., sufferings of various sorts. . . . Experiences, thoughts,—life can force this concept on us. (CV, p. 86)[5]

Sufferings due to a life-threatening illness or the death of a loved one may "sober up" a hedonistic person to the extent that he gives up his "Life's a beach" philosophy. Scriptural texts now speak to him for the first time and give him quite a different picture: "the Lord he is God; . . . we are his people, and the sheep of his pasture" (Psalm 100).

It is said that moving from a secular to an authentically religious life is more like a difficult leap than a comfortable walk. What is the particular difficulty of this proverbial "leap"? It is more a difficulty of the will than of the intellect (I want to say): it is more like when shy people risk contact with others than when reasonable people let down their guard and make shaky inferences with confidence. Genuine religious faith takes courage: if it were a matter of making shaky inferences with great confidence, it would call for foolhardiness rather than courage.[6]

Some would-be believers reject the theology presented to them because they see it as intellectually dishonest conjecture or speculation. If they come to see theology as a kind of grammar, however, that will open up the possibility that the real difficulty of committing themselves to the religion may lie elsewhere—in acknowledging a radical unsatisfactoriness in their present way

---

place in the development of religious doctrine. Think of how Jesus criticized the religion of the Pharisees and Scribes, Buddha the Brahminism of his time, Zen Buddhists the superstitious attachment to Buddhist words and images, etc.

5. This passage concludes with: "So perhaps ['God'] is similar to the concept of 'object.'" Compare: "What I called 'objects' were simply what we can speak about *no matter what may be the case*. Wouldn't it be absurd if someone asked me how I know *feet* exist after I had told him I'm 6 ft. tall?" (*PR*, p. 72, paraphrased). And compare: "Perhaps one could 'convince someone that God exists' by means of a certain kind of upbringing"(CV, p. 85)—as children are "convinced that feet and inches exist" in the course of learning their mother tongue. ("Object" is a grammatical category; "length," "color," "number," . . . and "God" are grammatical objects. God differs from other such objects in that any method for identifying, or measuring him is "excluded from language" (*PI*, sec. 500)—ruled out as heresy.

6. Compare Wittgenstein's remarks on courage in CV.

of life; in submitting to theological instruction in hopes of learning a better way. Such instruction, according to Wittgenstein, would have to be at once the description of a system of reference and an appeal to conscience:

> And this combination would have to result in the pupil himself . . . passionately taking hold of the system of reference. It would be as though someone were first to let me see the hopelessness of my situation and then show me the means of rescue until, of my own accord, or not at any rate led to it by my *instructor*, I ran to it and grasped it. (CV, p. 64)

Using Words in a Secondary Sense

We were able to express a number of experiences well before we learned to speak: for example, we reacted to an injury by crying and clutching the hurt part. As time went on, we learned to use "pain" and other conventional expressions to supplement these natural expressions of pain. It was the same with a number of other words for feelings. For example, we learned to use "amazement" and "wonder" to supplement characteristic facial expressions, gestures, and outcries of wonder and amazement.

Once in a lecture Wittgenstein described what he called his "experience *par excellence*" by saying: "when I have it *I wonder at the existence of the world*" (PO, p. 41). Then he proceeded to explain that he had just *misused* the word "wonder." Like the rest of us, he was taught to use it to express a reaction to the strange and unusual; here he is using it to express a reaction to whatever he looks at, however ordinary. "And I am then inclined to use such phrases as 'how extraordinary that anything should exist'" (ibid).[7]

As we learned English, we picked up the word God and learned to connect it with (among other phrases) "maker of the world." This was a deviation from the ordinary use of the word *maker*. We learned that God is the creator of the world—that is, the maker of what, in everyday speech, nobody made.

"Beavers made the dam" is a causal explanation. And although "God made the world," may be also, by analogy, a causal explanation, it is primarily (in terms of how it functions in our lives), the expression of an experience—the same experience originally expressed by the exclamation: "How extraordinary that the world should exist!"

---

7. This "misuse" of words in order to express an experience is a common phenomenon. A relatively trivial example is that of someone's spontaneously predicating *colors* of musical notes, or vowels—e.g., "For me *e* is yellow." Instead of calling this a misuse, one could call it a *secondary* use. "Yellow" is used primarily in descriptions of the visual appearance of objects; using it to express an experience—a spontaneous reaction to the letter "e," for example—would be a secondary use. (See *PI*, p. 216.)

"A mighty fortress," "our refuge and our strength" are other phrases that we were taught to connect with "God" and pictures of God. And some of us eventually came to use them to express what Wittgenstein called "the feeling of absolute safety":

> I mean the state of mind in which one is inclined to say "I am safe, nothing can injure me whatever happens."... [This experience]... has been described by saying that we feel safe in the hands of God. (PO, pp. 41–42)

This safety is not "just another kind of safety"—one that continues the series: financial safety, consumer safety, sexual safety, etc. Money, goods and services, health, etc. are "worldly things." "Feeling safe in the hands of God" shows itself in a certain attitude to *all* such things: the attitude, namely,

> that takes a particular matter seriously, but then at a particular point doesn't take it seriously after all.... In this way a person can say it is very serious that so-and-so died before he could finish a certain work; and that in another sense it doesn't matter at all. Here we use the words "in a profounder sense." (RC, pp. 58–59; cf. CV, p. 85)

"We know that all things work together for good to them that love God" (Paul). Based on evidence, this confidence would be contingent and hypothetical, not absolute and categorical. Then "God" would signify an object measured, not a measure. "[So] if there were evidence, this would in fact destroy the whole business" (LC, p. 56).

Recall the sections in *PI* on the phrases "absolute simplicity" (46) and "necessary existence" (50). Regarded as naming kinds of simplicity and existence (as "light" and "dark" name kinds of beer), they are metaphysical illusions. Regarded instead (along with "absolute safety") as "thrusts against the limits of language," they may be seen as religious challenges to lives of anxious yearning for indestructibility, safety.[8]

Using a Picture

Wittgenstein asked the students in one of his classes at Cambridge to suppose they had a friend who is going to China where they will never see him again. Suppose, he continued, that your friend now exclaims: "We might see one another after death." One of the students responded: "In this case, you might only mean that he expressed a certain attitude." "No," Wittgenstein retorted,

> it isn't the same as saying "I'm very fond of you"—and it may not be the same as saying anything else. It says what it says. Why

---

8. Pp. 74–75, above, are relevant here.

> should you be able to substitute anything else?/ . . . The whole
> *weight* may be in the picture. . . . When I say he's using a picture I'm
> merely making a *grammatical* remark: [What I say] can only be ver-
> ified by the consequences he does or does not draw. (*LC*, pp.
> 71–72)

If, in a matter-of-fact tone of voice, he draws the consequence we ought to
make practical preparations for when we meet after death, Wittgenstein
would likely withdraw his grammatical remark and wonder if he really understood the man. (When he thought he was using a picture, he thought his
words implied something deeper, less mundane.) Another illustration: When
a friend assures me that nothing is hidden from the eye of God, I assume he is
in a religious frame of mind and is using a picture. But if he proceeds to draw
conclusions about the probable color of the Eye and the shape of its eyebrow,
then my assumption is shaken: I doubt that he uses "the eye of God" to regu-
late for everything in all his life, doubt that the picture actually goes deep with
him.

    If it goes deep with us to say that God created the heavens and the earth,
are we not using these words to express a certain conception of the world as a
whole and of our place in it—one from which we draw consequences such as:
don't take ordinary things for granted; they are important in their own right,
not just relative to our desires?[9]

The Ontological Argument

    Philosophers since Hume and Kant have tended to regard the argu-
ments for the existence of God as failed attempts to prove the existence of
something. I believe that at least one of them can be usefully reinterpreted
along Wittgensteinian lines.

    Descartes's *Discourse on Method*, Part IV, contains the following state-
ment of what Kant named "the ontological argument":

> [Turning to] my idea of a perfect Being, I found that this included
> the existence of such a Being, in the same way as . . . the idea of a
> sphere includes the equidistance of all parts of its surface from the
> center . . .

Restating the argument in *Meditations*, Part V, Descartes says:

> I assuredly find in myself the idea of God—of a supremely perfect
> Being . . . and I clearly and distinctly understand that everlasting
> existence belongs to his nature. . . . [E]xistence can no more be

---

9. On the common impression that Wittgenstein is insinuating a reductive philosophy of religious belief, "expressivism," see Edelman's "Pointing Unknowingly," especially sec. IV.

taken away from the divine essence than . . . the idea of a valley can be taken away from the idea of a hill. So it is not less absurd to think of God (that is, a supremely perfect Being) lacking existence (that is, lacking a certain perfection), than to think of a hill without a valley.[10]

Prior to this stage of his meditations, Descartes had "assured himself of his own existence as a thinking being—a mind." With this assurance (the *Cogito, ergo sum*), he proceeded to examine the various ideas present to his mind, wondering whether any of the things they represent really exist. He soon came upon "the idea of a supremely perfect Being" and (with further meditation) came to see that "doubting the existence of such a Being" would makes no more sense than "doubting that the points on the surface of a sphere are equidistant from the center." For, just as by its very nature a sphere is a kind of solid (or a dog a kind of animal), so by its very nature a supremely perfect Being exists.

I would follow Hume and Kant in rejecting the ontological argument considered as a proof for the existence of something; I would not follow them in rejecting it absolutely. For, considered in another way, I think it it provides a valuable reminder of a most important aspect of the Jewish-Christian-Islamic concept of one transcendent God.

"God's essence is supposed to guarantee his existence—what this really means," Wittgenstein suggests, "is that what is here at issue is not the existence of something" (CV, p. 82). Following this suggestion, I would say that the real reason it makes no sense to wonder whether the idea of God depicts something that really exists is simply that it depicts nothing at all—neither an existent nor a nonexistent something.

Think of ideas as "pictures of objects."[11] The question whether a picture depicts something that actually exists makes sense for pictures of animals and other things in a way in which it makes no sense for pictures of God. This is so—following Wittgenstein's suggestion—because a picture of God (in contrast with a picture of a dog, a dinosaur, or a unicorn, for example) depicts neither an existent *nor* a nonexistent (extinct or fictional) object. And this distinguishes Descartes's God from the superhuman deities of Homer and Hesiod:

> There can be a description [or picture] of what it would be like if there were gods on Olympus—but not: "what it would be like if there were such a thing as God." And to say this is to determine the concept "God" more precisely. (CV, p. 82)

---

10. From Meditation Five (Anscombe and Geach translation).
11. A phrase from early in Descartes's Third Meditation.

(Just before those lines, Wittgenstein compared the reality of God with the reality of color. Developing that striking comparison, I would say that while the color system opens up a "logical space" for describing the appearance of objects, monotheistic systems open up a "logical space" for challenging false absolutes—as with Paul's critique of those who make their bellies their god.)

When such systems (as I understand them) permit "pictures of God," they stress that they are not pictures of someone in the sense in which pictures of Adam are pictures of someone; when they permit the everyday use of the noun *God*, they warn (in effect) that its use is not to be construed on the model of object and designation.[12] And the ethico-religious weight this rule can bear is clear from the example of a monotheistic religion in which generosity, gratitude, and selflessness are supposed to be central:

> Thus, when you give alms, sound no trumpet before you, as the hypocrites do. . . . Truly, I say to you, they have their reward. (*Matthew* 6:12)

If you seek your reward from human beings, you do not seek it from God; if you seek it from God, "your eye is simple" (*Mt* 6:22)—the one in need is the sole object of your concern. You are to be always mindful of God, of course. But if (in the words of Gareth Moore), "you fall prey to grammatical illusion, to the temptation to see 'God' as the name of somebody, then in order to get your reward from God, you must get it out of your head that there might be this supposed somebody around watching, from whom you might expect a reward."[13] For when Matthew speaks of a heavenly treasure, he is teaching a radically new way of life—a way of giving. It is the mark of idolatrous religion that it demands only a redirection of natural acquisitiveness.[14]

RELIGIONS, LANGUAGE, AND ETHICS

Buddhism and Christianity

Different as it is from names like "Charlie," the name "God" certainly is in some ways used like a word representing a person. This is important because it ties in with distinctively theistic practices such as prayer. But while it is

---

12. Recall that even so orthodox a theologian as Thomas Aquinas argued that God falls under no genus—not even "substance" (*Summa* I: q. 3, articles 5–6). Cf. Augustine's *Confessions* IV: 16.

13. Gareth Moore, o.p., *Believing in God*, p. 144.

14. Compare Gareth Moore, op. cit., pp. 164–166. I am much indebted to Moore's work.

important that theistic (e.g., Christian) and nontheistic (e.g., Theravada Buddhist) religious practices are different and informed by different "pictures," it is equally important that the *points* of the practices are sometimes analogous. Think of the grace before meals in which we thank "the King of the Universe" for the food at our table, for example. While gratitude cannot (grammatically) take this form in Theravada Buddhism, it takes analogous forms—as in the monks' practice of ceremonially begging their food from the laity. Both practices are expressions of humility. Both (I want to say) convey the message that no man is an island—not even if he has the money to buy all the food he wants, not even if he is a holy man who has renounced the world.

While the Buddha traces our suffering to the fact that we are clingers in a world of impermanence and advises us to "let go," St. Paul admonishes us to trust in the Lord and have no anxiety about anything. Though their pictures are very different, what they do with them is not. Though Paul would add something like "let God" to the Buddha's "let go," his intention would surely not be to cater (in a new way) to our clinging tendencies. He is teaching a way of *resisting* such powerful natural tendencies, a way in which prayer (not meditation) is central. And in prayer (the Our Father, for instance) "the whole *weight* may be in the picture" (*LC*, p. 72).[15]

Is everything expressible with the word *God* also expressible without it? I take it that Wittgenstein would respond here as he did to the parallel question, "[D]on't you at least say that everything that can be expressed by means of the word 'soul' can also be expressed somehow by means of words for the corporeal?":

> I do not say that. But if it were so—what would it amount to? For the words, and also what we point to in explaining them, are nothing but instruments, and everything depends on their use. (*RPP-I*, sec. 586)[16]

The word *God*, and the picture of a great and powerful Lord pointed to in explaining it, are nothing but instruments, and everything depends on their

---

15. "We easily forget how much a . . . form of expression may mean to us" (*BB*, p. 57). (See Diamond's "The Dog That Gave Himself the Moral Law" for a fascinating application of this point to "the divine command" form of expression in ethics.) We also easily forget how different forms of expression can provoke characteristically different abuses. (While Christian talk of needing God's help is readily perverted into an excuse for moral passivity, Buddhist talk of working out one's own salvation readily becomes an ally of spiritual pride.)

16. This important remark was quoted more fully on pp. 108–109.

use. For example, consider their use in modifying our reaction to successfully overcoming "overwhelming obstacles." Where before we would have said, "Nobody helped us; so we must be stronger than we thought!," now we say, "God helped us!"

Although the sentences "God helped us" and "Nobody helped us" may be used in precisely the same circumstances, they are not to be construed as just two ways of saying the same thing. For they have completely different uses—the first to express a reaction to a situation, the second to describe it. Similarly: although what we point to in explaining what "blue" means in "That's a blue note" may be the same as what we point to in explaining what it means in "That's a blue flower," the two sentences have completely different uses—the first to express a reaction, the second to describe something.

In speaking of God's help, Christians (some Christians) are taking a word with an everyday meaning and giving it a secondary application—just the sort of thing jazz musicians do in speaking of blue notes. Could they express what they want to express without the color word? Could those who thank God for his help express the same thing without the word "help" or a synonym? I would be inclined to say: "Not the same thing; perhaps something analogous."

Christians and Buddhists obviously think differently in the sense that they "use different pictures." However (and this is a caveat Wittgenstein would want to stress), it is not always so clear they believe different things. A Buddhist telling a Christian "I don't believe in God" may only mean "I don't use pictures like 'Lord of the Universe' or anything that hangs together with them"; he may not be contradicting the Christian at all.

> [Here] you might say: "Well, if you can't contradict him, that means you don't understand him. If you did understand him, then you might." That again is Greek to me. My normal technique of language leaves me. I don't know whether to say they understand one another or not. (*LC*, p. 55)

What is to *count* as "understanding one another" here?

> Actually I should like to say that in this case too the *words* you utter or what you think as you utter them are not what matters, so much as the difference they make at various points in your life. . . . A theology which insists on the use of *certain particular* words and phrases, and outlaws others . . . gesticulates with words, as one might say, because it wants to say something and does not know how to express it. *Practice* gives the words their sense. (*CV*, p. 85)

"For," to repeat an earlier quote, "the words, and also what we point to in explaining them, are nothing but instruments, and everything depends on their use."[17]

Language and Religion

Although there are (for example) Christian and Buddhist language games, there is not (as far as I can see) a religious language game as such. Not itself a language game, religion is a spirit that can pervade (or be absent from) any and all language games. This is a point I first proposed at the beginning of my study of the *Investigations*; now, near the conclusion of the book, I want to explain it in terms of a poem (in my prose translation) by the nineteenth-century German romantic, Ludwig Uhland:

> Count Eberhard's Hawthorne
> On a pious journey to the shores of Palestine, the bearded Count Eberhard of Wittenberg snipped a green twig from a hawthorne tree while riding through a forest in early spring. Carefully placing it in his iron helmet, he wore it in battle and over the sea.
>
> When he returned home he placed it in the earth, where the mild spring awakened new shoots. Visiting it year after year, the good and faithful count rejoiced at how bravely it had grown.
>
> Now an old man, and the little twig a tree, the lord often sits beneath it in deep reverie. The soft rustle of its high, broad canopy takes him back to the old days and distant land.[18]

None of Uhland's sentences say anything particularly deep, none of his words are conventionally religious. And yet (I want to say) his poem is deeply religious. It sketches the old count's life "under the aspect of eternity," with a hawthorne tree at its center; it shows how that particular tree enabled one pious individual to "stand back from his world" ("his life in space and time") and see it as a limited, meaningful whole.[19]

---

17. Imagining concepts *essentially* different from our own requires imagining people whose life would run on quite differently from our own: "What interest us would not interest *them* . . ." (Z, sec. 388).

18. Wittgenstein's friend Paul Engelmann quotes the German original and Wittgenstein's reaction to it in *Letters*, pp. 82–85.

19. As a pious Christian, the count would also have experienced the hawthorne as emblematic of the Tree of Life in Genesis and the Tree of the Cross in the Gospels. Had he been a pious Buddhist rather than a Christian crusader, it would doubtless have been emblematic of the Bodhi Tree./ On "aspect of eternity," see NB, p.51 and CV, pp. 4–5. Edelman equates it, plausibly, with "seeing things apart from our own contingent interests" ("Beauty," p. 11).

Although the hawthorne was Eberhard's personal channel of grace, anything might become so to an individual or to a people:

> [A]nd the characteristic feature of the awakening mind of man is
> precisely the fact that a phenomenon comes to have meaning for
> him. One could almost say that man is a ceremonial animal. (*PO*,
> p. 129)

One could add, I think, that religious ceremonies and beliefs are among the
oldest expressions of the characteristically human practice of taking over
equipment, actions, and words from everyday (secular, prosaic) life and giving
them "secondary," ceremonial-expressive uses.

Religion and Ethics

Some Buddhists have criticized John Paul II's recent book for denying the
Buddha a place on the same spiritual level with Christ. One response would be
to compare the pope's role vis-à-vis Catholic piety to that of the Académie
Francaise vis-à-vis the French language and say that what these Buddhists perceive as arrogance may only be an exercise of his official role as guardian of the
Catholic language game. That would not be a response likely to satisfy orthodox Catholics, however. For while they can (and should) respect different
religious traditions, they surely cannot regard them as "equally good."[20]

If orthodox Catholics think Buddhists must be missing something
important, it seems they would think Benthamites, Comptean positivists,
Marxists, and Nietzscheans (for example) must be missing even more.
Speaking for myself, I think the most important difference here would be a difference in the values by which the different believers assess their lives.

"Suppose I say Christian ethics is right," asks Wittgenstein, comparing
it with a Nietzschean system:

> Then I am making a judgment of value. It amounts to adopting
> Christian ethics. It is not like saying that one of these physical the-
> ories must be the right one. The way in which some reality corre-
> sponds—or conflicts—with a physical theory has no counterpart
> here.

That we should not read a form of relativism into the preceding lines is clear, I
think, from the paragraph following them:

> If you say there are various systems of ethics you are not saying they
> are all equally right. This means nothing. Just as it would have no

---

20. They might take a page from Kierkegaard's *Philosophical Fragments* and argue that,
like Socrates, the Buddha was a great teacher but not the "present help and savior" we
need. Compare *CV*, p. 33 (on the Resurrection).

meaning to say that each was right from his own standpoint. That
could only mean that each judges as he does.[21]

"Each judges as he judges" is a tautology and therefore says nothing. But is
there truth or falsity in the way a man judges? An ethical system certainly does
not conform or conflict with reality *in the way* a physical theory conforms or
conflicts with reality. Is there another way?

To vary the theme of the final section of "Arithmetic as Grammar": the
"conformity to reality" of an ethical system is not to be compared with the
"conformity to data" said to confirm a physical theory; it is to be compared,
rather, with the meaningfulness of the concepts articulated in the system, as
exhibited by their use-in-practice.

A philosophical investigation of "the reality behind an ethical system"
might begin by asking what it would be like for its associated concepts to drop
out of use. Suppose we no longer find any real use in practice for any weighty
distinction between, for example: lust and sexual desire; temperance and con-
tinence; rational and irrational appetite; human being (*Mensch*) and member
of the species *homo sapiens*: what, if anything, would be lost or gained? Suppose
(to generalize) that a "more nuanced" ethical system (an Aristotelian virtue
ethics, for example) gets elbowed out of our thinking by a newer, "more
streamlined" system (such as Bentham's utilitarianism): would such a change
be an *impoverishment*—a significant loss of ready-to-hand resources of thought
and expression?

I will not proceed to the detailed investigation a just response to those
questions would demand.[22] Instead (and in keeping with the more synoptic
aim of this book), I will respond briefly to another question: What would it be
like to abandon serious moral thinking altogether? What (in other words)
would a *general* rejection of moral concepts look like in practice?

Imagine coming across someone who claims to believe that everything
we might call moral values (compassion, fairness, generosity, etc.) is really
bad, and who maintains that anybody who says otherwise is either stupid or
hypocritical. It is obvious to any person of sense, he says, that the only thing
intrinsically good is satisfying one's own desires; compassionate, generous
behavior is at best, in his view, means to an end—e.g., means to win the assis-
tance of other people and keep out of jail. Would a choice between this
amoral point of view and a moral point of view have to be described as *arbi-*

21. Rush Rhees, "Some Developments," p. 24. (Rhees is reporting something
Wittgenstein had said in conversation.)
22. Cora Diamond makes significant contributions to such an investigation in "Losing
Your Concepts," an essay to which I am much indebted.

trary? Can we answer this Thrasymachean (Nietzschean?) someone without descending into logical fallacy or rhetorical diatribe?

Guided by the way Charles Dickens awakened the conscience of his readers in *Oliver Twist* and *A Christmas Carol*, my response would be to tell him stories that exemplify the sort of life issues involved. I would then add remarks in the spirit of the following passage from Cyril Barrett:

> [Ethical value can be] shown, but not stated or described as we describe the weight, shape, and size of a cannonball. But how do we *show* ethical value? By examples . . . / Suppose you are asked whether it is wrong to kill innocent people because they do not fit into our culture and ethos, and your reply is that it is not only wrong but a vile and dastardly thing to do. Now suppose you are asked what evidence you have for this course of action to be wrong. What would your reaction be? Something from bewilderment to indignation, I should hope.[23]

Without wanting to attribute it to Barrett or to Wittgenstein, I would add the analogy: "Justifying ethical values with evidence" would be like "illuminating the sun with searchlights." It is in the light of ethical values that we perceive the vileness in some of our desires and projects—as (to introduce another analogy) it is in the light of logical principles that we perceive the invalidity in some of our inferences.

Suppose someone challenged the validity of *modus ponens*. What would he be looking for? A truth-table proof? That would be circular: *modus ponens*-style inference is required for reading the truth table.[24] An inductive, empirical proof (a "decisive experiment" in support of a physical theory)? That would be irrelevant: *modus ponens* is a form of *deductive* inference. The appropriate response, I think, would be to make sure he understands what would be at stake in rejecting *modus ponens* in practice. And we could do this by giving examples. Now suppose someone challenged a formulation of elementary morality or "common decency" such as the Golden Rule. What would he be looking for? Wouldn't his challenge call for a comparable investigation?

Ethical Problems

An ethical problem is the expression of a conflict or disharmony: either there are conflicting commitments and demands without any obvious way of resolving them, or a tension between duty and inclination. We want to do justice to all the various goods, norms, commitments, and ideals of common life and

---

23. Barrett, *Wittgenstein*, pp. 234–236, paraphrased. Compare his article on ethics and aesthetics, especially sec. IV.

24. Explained in my *Logic*, pp. 86 (question m) and 189.

practice, but find that "principles of common decency" such as the Golden Rule provide no decisive guidance in harmonizing them.

Consider the following example. Marriage entails certain responsibilities and one's career entails others. Suppose a man comes to the conclusion he must either leave his wife or abandon his work of cancer research. Perhaps he has a deep love for her but thinks that giving up his work would drag them both down. God help him, we might say: whatever he finally does, he may later regret. He is facing the profoundest of questions—what sort of life to live, what sort of person to become.

Wittgenstein used that example to illustrate what he understood by an ethical problem and its solution. Solving such a problem amounts to changing one's way of living and assessing life in such a way that the conflict is resolved.[25]

Someone with an authentic faith in a particular religion or wisdom tradition has, in effect, already decided what sort of life to lead. He brings an overall ethical perspective to bear on the conflicting responsibilities he experiences in his life. If he is a Christian of a certain sort, then, faced with a choice between his wife and career, he would regard the question, "Should I leave her?" not as a problem to be solved, but as a temptation to be resisted. For him the real ethical problem would be: "how to make the best of this situation, what to do in order to be a decent husband for her in these greatly altered circumstances" (Rhees, p. 23).

But problems keep coming up that threaten the balance anew, problems that challenge the solutions we found for ourselves (with or without the aid of a religion or wisdom tradition). And while we may continue to take these problems and solutions seriously, we may also come to regard something else as even more serious. For example, we may conclude that while abandoning a promising career of cancer research is in one sense a very regrettable matter, in another it doesn't matter at all: "At this point one uses the words 'in a deeper sense'" (CV, p. 85).[26]

In 1929 Wittgenstein summed up his own ethical position in the words "What is good is also divine" (CV, p. 3). But what would such an ethics entail? I suggest that it would entail relativizing *all* one's problems and solutions— even those sanctioned by the ethico-religious system to which one may be

---

25. Much of the material from this section, including the preceding example, comes from Rhees, "Some Developments in Wittgenstein's View of Ethics." I am also indebted to the John C. Kelly article mentioned in the bibliography.

26. Here I think of how the venerable doctrine of "divine simplicity" suggests that the many perfections we talk about in daily life (justice, mercy, etc.) are—"in a deeper sense," in God—only one.

committed. This would be to acknowledge a distance between religion as part of the traffic of human life and language, and religion as "the calm bottom of the sea at its deepest point, which remains calm however high the waves on the surface may be" (CV, p. 53; cf. *Matthew* 25: 32–40).

Those on this "calm bottom" do not experience life as a tragedy. Nor do they go along with the Nietzschean conception of hardness and conflict as something splendid. For they do not experience the problem of life as a problem: it is for them "a bright halo round . . . life, not a dubious background" (CV, p. 27).

The preface to the *Tractatus* concluded by saying that the value of the work, if any, consists of two things: first that it solves the problems of philosophy in all essentials, second that "it shows how little is achieved when these problems are solved" (p. 4). Although Wittgenstein could not have made the first point about any of his later writings, I believe he could have made the second. For I think he continued to regard the most important things in life as essentially "outside the city limits of language,"[27] and all possible problems and solutions (in philosophy or elsewhere) as within them:

> Is not this the reason why those who have found after a long period
> of doubt that the sense of life became clear to them have then been
> unable to say what constituted that sense? (*TLP*, 6.521)

Although they find that nothing they can say explains that sense, they may still want to give it linguistic expression. They may say of some combinations of words ("safe in the hands of God," for instance): to us, they say something of transcendent significance, though we can put nothing side by side with them to serve as explanations. The point is not that language is limited or our vocabulary inadequate. The point is that we do not want to put anything "side by side" with those words, and would exclude any proffered explanation precisely because it was an explanation.

"Language is, after all, not a cage" (*WVC*, p. 117). Nor is it always what we want.[28]

---

27. Compare "language and the activities into which it is woven" with the "flourishing colonial system on the coast, the interior still wilderness" mentioned on p. 10, above. Judging from memoirs, etc., it appears that Wittgenstein's personal faith was that—when all is said and done—salvation is to be found in that "interior wilderness." (See CV: pp. 1 h, 6 b, 9 c, and 14 c.)

28. Recall my comments on indescribability (pp. 74–75) and "the compass user" (p. 40). Drawing on that material, I would contrast the *Wittgensteinian mystic*—who might talk of "hearkening to an inspiration" in what he does and the words he uses, with the *private language mystic*—who might talk of "following a private rule."

CHAPTER SIX

Conclusion

The problems arising through a misinterpretation of our forms of language . . . . are deep disquietudes; their roots are as deep in us as the forms of our language . . .

—*Philosophical Investigations*, sec. 111

PHILOSOPHY AND THE YEARNING FOR THE TRANSCENDENT

"A Deep Disquietude"
(PI, Section 111)

As long as there continues to be a verb "to be" that looks as if it functions in the same way as "to eat" . . . etc. etc., people will keep stumbling over the same puzzling difficulties. . . . (CV, p. 15)

If a tradition of conceptual puzzlement and investigation is counted the most distinctive feature of Western philosophy, then Parmenides of Elea, not Thales of Miletus, is "father of Western philosophy." The heart of the argument in Parmenides' *Way of Truth* is that since every thought is *about* something, no thought is about what has yet to exist or ceased to exist, for then—absurdly—it would be about nothing.[1] Parmenides assumes that an object of thought must always *exist*. And while few post-Eleatic philosophers fully endorsed the "static monism" to which Parmenides' reasoning seemed to lead, many shared his assumption. One such philosopher was Wittgenstein's great mentor, Bertrand Russell.

---

1. I believe my interpretation of Parmenides is fairly standard. See, e.g., Allen, ed., *Greek Philosophy*, p. 13. And compare Wittgenstein's *PI*, sec. 518 account of a similar argument in Plato's *Theaetetus*.

In Russell's account, Parmenides was the first to make it clear that "if we can use a word intelligibly, it must have some meaning, and what it means must exist in some sense or other."[2] But while Russell considered this an important point, he certainly did not want to accept Parmenides' paradoxical conclusion that coming to be, perishing, and multiplicity are illusions. He reasoned that we must be speaking loosely when we say we're thinking of (for instance) George Washington, who no longer exists: for although there is (and must be) *something* for "G.W." (or any functioning name) to mean, that "something" cannot now be G.W. What is it then? Russell concluded that when we think of G.W., we must be thinking of some representation of him: "We may think of his picture, and say to ourselves, 'Yes, that man.' [Or] we may think 'the first President of the United States.' "[3]

The obvious objection to Russell's response is that thinking of G.W. is quite a different thing from thinking of his representation. When the object of a thought is a representation, asking how accurate it is makes sense; when it is a person, it does not. A picture has a style and a subject in a way a person does not, etc.

We find a less objectionable response to Parmenides when we approach names and thoughts with no assumption about *what has to be so* for them to have meaning. We will then look at how the words *name* and *thought* actually function in our language. Compare: (1) "You are pointing at a dodo bird" with (2) "You are thinking of a dodo bird."[4] Proposition *1* entails the existence of at least one dodo bird; proposition *2* does not. *1* and *2* have the same surface grammar (verb-prepositional phrase); they have different depth grammars—they are used in two different language games. If we approach language determined to use *1* as the model for understanding *2*, we will be forced into the paradoxical claims of Parmenides or one of his philosophical progeny. We need to change our approach. Someone claims to be thinking of dodo birds. In ordinary life no one would suppose that determining whether dodos exist would be relevant to verifying that claim. Suppose he had been, for example, drawing dodo pictures or using the word "dodo" in telling a story—*these* are the sorts of things that would be relevant to verifying his claim.[5]

It might be objected: "Since G.W. is the object of my thought and G.W. doesn't exist, the object of my thought does not exist. And isn't this conclusion absurd?" Indeed, it does make perfectly good sense in ordinary English to

---

2. *Wisdom of the West*, p. 29.

3. *A History of Western Philosophy*, p. 51.

4. Cf. *PI*, secs. 462 and 464.

5. On meaning and verification, see pp. 55–56, above.

say that one is thinking of somebody who no longer exists. But the critic is uncomfortable and dissatisfied with this feature of ordinary language, for it appears to him to imply that one is thinking of something and yet thinking of nothing—which certainly is absurd. To that objection, the appropriate reply is to remind the critic of relevant linguistic commonplaces—for example, that in everyday linguistic interchange we would not accept the fact of G.W.'s present nonexistence as evidence for the statement "So-and-so [who has just uttered the first president's name] is thinking of nothing." For *that* judgment, relevant evidence would be (for instance) that So-and-so is drugged and doesn't respond to questions.

Though perhaps "the only strictly correct" kind of response to philosophers in the tradition of Parmenides, the foregoing reply will not satisfy them—will not satisfy *us*. It is not deep enough, we want to say. (Compare the *Tractatus*:

> The correct method in philosophy would really be to say nothing but what can be said, . . . and then to show to anyone wanting to say something metaphysical that he has failed to assign meaning to some of the signs in his sentences. Although he wouldn't find this method satisfying [he wouldn't feel like we're teaching him philosophy], *it* would be the only strictly correct one.[6])

To be really satisfied, really at peace, we must come to see our discomfort with ordinary language in a new way, under a fresh, liberating aspect. Perhaps it will only be after "long and involved journeyings" (*PI*, p. v) that it truly dawns on us that—as with Augustine's "philosophical concept of meaning"— Parmenides' assumption "has its place in a primitive idea of the way language functions" (*PI*, sec. 2).

"Running Up Against the Limits" (PI, Section 119)

We are still occupied by the same philosophical problems as were the ancients. Why? Because our language has remained fundamentally the same:

> [A]s long as we continue to talk of a river of time, of an expanse of space, etc., etc., people will keep stumbling over the same puzzling difficulties and find themselves staring at something which no explanation seems capable of clearing up. (*CV*, p. 15)

---

6. *TLP*, 6.54, in my—somewhat free—translation. The article by Conant mentioned in the bibliography presents a most illuminating interpretation of this and related passages.

But if intelligent people learn from experience, why do philosophers keep on philosophizing? Because the stumbling the philosophizing occasions

> . . . satisfies a longing for the transcendent, because in so far as peo-
> ple think they can see the "limits of human understanding," they
> believe of course that they can see beyond these. (CV, p. 15)

What, then, becomes of philosophy once philosophers have seen through that illusion?

According to the *Tractatus*, the proper business of philosophy is that of drawing a limit to thought

> or rather—not to thought, but to the expression of thoughts: for in
> order to be able to draw a limit to thought, we should have to find
> both sides of the limit thinkable (i.e. we should have to be able to
> think what cannot be thought). (*TLP*, p. 3)

So what philosophy discovers is a limit, not of thought or human understanding, but of language: for it will "only be in language that the limit can be drawn, and what lies on the other side of the limit will simply be nonsense" (ibid.). In other words:

> The results of philosophy are the uncovering of one or another
> piece of plain nonsense and of bumps that the understanding has
> got by running its head up against the limits of language. These
> bumps make us see the value of the discovery. (*PI*, sec. 119)

It is by "running up against them" that we discover these limits. We are then in a position to sketch their contours, with a view to "the logical clarification of thoughts" (*TLP*, 4.112). And now we see that the true value of philosophy lies is in this clarificatory activity itself, not in any special power it has to satisfy our longings for the transcendent.

"The Problem of Life"
(TLP, 6.521)

The experience of life as an essentially frustrating "vanity of vanities" may end in despair. Or it may lead to yearning for the transcendent. This yearning also may end badly—in illusory satisfactions and new despair; or it may end well, with its only real solution: "the vanishing of the problem" (*TLP*, 6.521). Buddhism calls this vanishing of yearning *nirvana*, Hinduism "renunciation of the fruits of action," Biblical religions "the peace of the God" or "kingdom of heaven."

"Transcendent" does not name one kind of object of yearning among others. When we yearn for an object and get it, that is our reward. We get our transcendent reward, however, only after we stop acting for the sake of reward.

Therefore, the transcendent is not just another object of desire—not something "*within* space and time."

We solve "the riddle of life in space and time" (*TLP*, 6.4312) not by retreating from life but by living it in a new way: not for the sake of rewards, but "to the glory of God." So lived, life ceases to seem essentially problematic.[7]

"*The Real Discovery*"
(*PI*, Section 133)

In some the yearning for knowledge is paramount—they become scientists. When scientists come to feel that no possible advance in scientific knowledge will satisfy their yearning, they may turn to philosophy.

"Philosophy aims at the logical clarification of thoughts" (*TLP*, 4.112). When it does not rest in its "merely clarificatory" activity, it turns into metaphysics. Metaphysics (to use Kant's distinction) is either transcendental or transcendent: transcendental if it seeks to unearth an "*a priori* order of the world" (*PI*, sec. 97), transcendent if it "believes it can see beyond" that order (*CV*, p. 15). Our real need as philosophers is to leave off *both* forms of metaphysics.[8] Then we discover that solving the problems that concern us requires no "*penetration* of phenomena" (*PI*, sec. 90), metaphysical or otherwise. Understanding that "what is hidden is of no interest to us," we are finally content with a philosophy that "neither explains nor deduces anything" (*PI*, sec. 126).

Philosophical problems are to be solved by arranging what we have always known about our language and the actions into which it is woven.[9] Problems: they are not to be "rolled up into one overwhelming question":

> —Instead, we now demonstrate a method, by examples; and the series of examples can be broken off.—Problems are solved (difficulties eliminated), not a *single* problem. (*PI*, sec. 133)

As with "the solution of the problem of life" in *Tractatus* 6.521, the solution of that "*single* problem" is seen in its vanishing.

---

7. See *CV*, pp. 14 c and 27 d. On the previous line, see p. 11, above, and *Bhagavad Gita* 18: 6.

8. To make a very long story short: Kant practiced and was comfortable with transcendental metaphysics; *TLP* (climaxing at proposition 6) practiced that form of metaphysics but was not comfortable with it (*TLP*, 6.53–7); *PI* decisively rejects metaphysics in any form as inessential—and detrimental—to the philosopher's "real need" (*PI*, sec. 108). For more on these matters, see Diamond's *Realistic Spirit*, pp. 13–38. Cf. *CV*, p. 7: "Anything that I might reach by climbing a ladder does not interest me" (dated 1930).

9. Based on *PI*, secs. 7 d and 109.

Bibliography

Anscombe, G.E.M. and Peter Geach, eds. and trs. *Descartes: Philosophical Writings*. New York: Bobbs-Merrill, 1971.

Allen, Reginald, ed. *The Greek Philosophers*. New York: The Free Press, 1985.

Aquinas, St. Thomas. *Summa Theologiae*, Vol. I. Thomas Gilby, ed. New York: Image Books, 1969.

Augustine, St. *The Confessions*. Rex Warner, trans. New York: Mentor Books, 1963.

Barrett, Cyril. *Wittgenstein on Ethics and Religious Belief*. Oxford: Blackwell, 1991.

———. "'(Ethics and Aesthetics are One),'" in *Aesthetics*, Proceeedings of the 8th International Wittgenstein Symposium. Vienna: Hölder-Pichler-Tempsky, 1984, pp. 17–22.

Berkeley, George. *Three Dialogues Between Hylas and Philonous*. Indianapolis: Bobbs-Merrill, 1954.

Benardette, José A. "Real Definitions, Quine, and Aristotle." *Philosophical Studies* 72 (1993): pp. 265–282.

Bouwsma, O.K. *Wittgenstein: Conversations, 1949–1951*. Edited with an introduction by J.L. Craft and Ronald E. Hustwit. Indianapolis: Hackett, 1986.

Brenner, William H. "'Brownish Yellow' and 'Reddish Green.'" *Philosophical Investigations* 10 (1987), pp. 200–211.

———. "Chesterton, Wittgenstein, and the Foundations of Ethics." *Philosophical Investigations* 14 (1991): pp. 311–323.

———. *Logic and Philosophy: An Integrated Introduction*. Notre Dame, Ind.: University of Notre Dame Press, 1993.

———. "Seeing Red Blue." In *Wittgenstein: Towards a Re-Evaluation*. Rudolf Haller, ed. Vienna: Hölder-Pichler-Temsky, 1990, pp. 250–253.

———. "Wittgenstein's Color Grammar." *The Southern Journal of Philosophy* 20 (1982): pp. 289–298.

———. "Theology as Grammar" *The Southern Journal of Philosophy* 34 (1996): pp. 439–454.

————. "The Soulless Tribe." *The Southern Journal of Philosophy* 33 (1995): pp. 279–298.

————. "Arithmetic as Grammar." *Philosophical Investigations* 20 (1997): pp. 315–325.

Cavell, Stanley. *The Claim of Reason*. New York: Oxford University Press, 1979.

Champlin, T.S. "Head Colds and Thoughts in the Head." *Philosophy* 68 (1989): pp. 39–48.

Conant, James. "Throwing Away the Top of the Ladder." *Yale Review* 79 (1989–1990): pp. 328–364.

Dennett, Daniel. *Darwin's Dangerous Idea*. New York: Simon and Schuster, 1995.

Diamond, Cora. "Losing Your Concepts." *Ethics* 98 (1988): pp. 255–277.

————. *The Realistic Spirit: Wittgenstein, Philosophy, and the Mind*. Cambridge, Mass.: MIT Press, 1991.

————. "Wittgenstein, Mathematics, and Ethics: Resisting the Attractions of Realism." In *The Cambridge Companion to Wittgenstein*. Hans Sluga and David G. Stern, eds. New York: Cambridge University Press, 1996.

————. "The Dog that Gave Himself the Moral Law." *Midwest Studies in Philosophy* 13 (1988): pp. 161–179.

Edelman, John T. "Beauty and the Attainment of Temperance." *International Philosophical Quarterly* 37 (1997): pp. 5–12.

————. "Humanity, Authority, and the Mesmeric Ought." *Philosophical Investigations* 20 (1997): pp. 326–346.

————. *An Audience For Moral Philosophy*. London: Macmillan, 1991.

————. "Pointing Unknowingly: Fantasy, Nonsense, and 'Religious Understanding.'" *Philosophical Investigations* 21 (1998): pp. 63–87.

Engelmann, Paul. *Letters From Ludwig Wittgenstein, With a Memoir*. Oxford: Blackwell, 1967. Translated by L. Furtmüller, edited by B. F. McGuinness.

Fann, K.T., ed. *Ludwig Wittgenstein: the Man and His Philosophy*. New York: Dell, 1967.

Fingarettet, Herbert. *Confucius—the Secular as Sacred*. New York: Harper and Row, 1972.

Fieguth, Gerhard, ed. *Deutsche Aphorismen*. Stuttgart: Reclam, 1978.

Foot, Philippa. "Moral Beliefs." *Proceedings of the Aristotelian Society* for 1958–59 (and frequently anthologized).

Fleming, Noel. "Seeing the Soul." *Philosophy* 53 (1978): pp. 33–50.

Frege, Gottlob. "The Thought: A Logical Inquiry," translated by A.M. and M. Quinton. In *Philosophical Logic*. P.F. Strawson, ed. New York: Oxford University Press, 1969.

Garfield, Jay L. *The Fundamental Wisdom of the Middle Way*. New York: Oxford, 1995.

Gier, Nicholas. *Wittgenstein and Phenomenology*. Albany, N.Y.: SUNY Press, 1981.

Goethe, Johann Wolfgang von. *Theory of Colors* (*Zur Farbenlehre*). Cambridge, Mass.: MIT Press, 1970. (Reprint of C. L. Eastlake's 1840 translation.)

Hacker, P.M.S. *Wittgenstein: Meaning and Mind*. Cambridge, Mass.: Blackwell, 1990.

Hacker, P.M.S., and G.P. Baker. *Wittgenstein: Rules, Grammar, and Necessity*. New York: Blackwell, 1985.

———. *Wittgenstein: Understanding and Meaning*. Chicago: University of Chicago Press, 1980.

Hallett, Garth L. *A Companion to Wittgenstein's 'Philosophical Investigations'*. Ithaca: Cornell University Press, 1977.

———. *Christian Moral Reasoning: An Analytic Guide*. Notre Dame, Ind.: University of Notre Dame Press, 1983.

Hanfling, Oswald. *Language and the Privacy of Experience*. Milton Keynes, England: Open University Press, 1976.

———. *Wittgenstein's Later Philosophy*. Albany, N.Y.: SUNY Press, 1989.

———. *Logical Positivism*. New York: Columbia University Press, 1981.

Hatab, Lawrence J., and William Brenner. "Heidegger and Wittgenstein on Language and Mystery." *International Studies in Philosophy* 15 (1983): pp. 25–43.

Harris, C. Edwin, Jr. "The Problem of Induction in the Later Wittgenstein." *Southwestern Journal of Philosophy* 3 (1972): pp. 135–146.

Heidegger, Martin, and Eugen Fink. *Heraclitus Seminar, 1966/67*. University, Alabama: The University of Alabama Press, 1979.

Heidegger, Martin. *Basic Writings*. David Farrell Krell, ed. New York: Harper and Row, 1977.

Johnston, Paul. *Rethinking the Inner*. New York: Routledge, 1993.

———. *Wittgenstein and Moral Philosophy*. New York: Routledge, 1989.

Jones, J.R. "Love as Perception of Meaning." In *Religion and Understanding*. D.Z. Phillips, ed. Oxford: Blackwell, 1967.

Kelly, John C. "Wittgenstein, the Self, and Ethics." *Review of Metaphysics* 48 (1995): pp. 567–590.

Koch, Kenneth. "The Language of Poetry." *New York Review of Books*, May 14, 1998: pp. 44–47.

Lear, Jonathan. "Leaving the World Alone." *The Journal of Philosophy* 79 (1982): pp. 382–403.

Malcolm, Norman. *Ludwig Wittgenstein: A Memoir*, 2nd ed. New York: Oxford, 1984.

———. *Problems of Mind*. New York: Harper, 1971.

———. "Review of 'Philosophical Investigations.'" *Philosophical Review* 63 (1954): pp. 530–559.

———. *Thought and Knowledge*. Ithaca: Cornell University Press, 1977.

Mulhall, Steven. *On Being in the World: Wittgenstein and Heidegger on Seeing Aspects*. New York: Routledge, 1990.

Moore, Gareth, o.p. *Believing in God: A Philosophical Essay*. Edinburgh: T & T Clark, 1988.

Mounce, H.O. *Wittgenstein's Tractatus: An Introduction*. Chicago: University of Chicago Press, 1981.

———. "Review of *Remarks on Color*." *Philosophical Quarterly* 30 (1980): pp. 159–160.

Murdoch, Iris. *Metaphysics as a Guide to Morals*. New York: Penguin, 1993.

Quine, Willard Van Orman. *From a Logical Point of View: Logico-Philosophical Essays*, 2nd ed., revised. New York: Harper, 1963.

Rhees, Rush. "Some Developments in Wittgenstein's View of Ethics." *Philosophical Review* 74 (1965): pp. 17–26.

———. "The Language of Sense Data and Private Experience. (Notes taken by Rush Rhees of Wittgenstein's Lectures, 1936." *Philosophical Investigations* 7 (1984).

Richter, Duncan. "Nothing To Be Said: Wittgenstein and Wittgensteinian Ethics." *The Southern Journal of Philosophy* 34 (1996): pp. 243–256.

Ryle, Gilbert. *The Concept of Mind*. London: Hutchinson, 1949.

Russell, Bertrand. *A History of Western Philosophy*. New York: Simon and Schuster, 1945.

————. "The Philosophy of Logical Atomism." In (for example) *Logic and Knowledge*. R.C. Marsh, ed. London: Allen and Unwin, 1956.

————. *Wisdom of the West*. Garden City, N. Y.: Doubleday, 1959.

Sass, Louis A. *The Paradoxes of Delusion: Wittgenstein, Schreber and the Schizophrenic Mind*. Ithaca: Cornell University Press, 1994.

Schulte, Joachim. *Experience and Expression: Wittgenstein's Philosophy of Psychology*. New York: Oxford University Press, 1993.

————. *Wittgenstein: Eine Einführung*. Stuttgart: Reclam, 1989.

————. *Wittgenstein: An Introduction*. William H. Brenner and John F. Holley, trans. Albany, N.Y.: SUNY Press, 1992.

Sluga, Hans. *Heidegger's Crisis: Philosophy and Politics in Nazi Germany*. Cambridge: Harvard University Press, 1993.

Sraffa, Piero. *Production of Commodities by Means of Commodities*. Cambridge: Cambridge University Press, 1960.

Stern, David G. *Wittgenstein on Mind and Language*. New York: Oxford University Press, 1995.

Teghrarian, S., and A. Serafini, eds. *Wittgenstein and Contemporary Philosophy*. Wakefield, New Hampshire: Longwood Academic, 1992.

Thurman, Robert A.F. *The Central Philosophy of Tibet*. Princeton: Princeton University Press, 1984.

Toulmin, Stephen. "The Marginal Relevance of Theory in the Humanities." *Common Knowledge* 1993: pp. 75–84.

Vesey, Godfrey, ed. *Understanding Wittgenstein*. Ithaca: Cornell University Press, 1974.

Waismann, Friedrich. *Principles of Linguistic Philosophy*. R. Harré, ed. New York: St. Martin's Press, 1965.

Weil, Simone. *Waiting for God*. New York: Harper, 1973.

————. *Gravity and Grace*. London: Routledge and Kegan Paul, 1963.

Wheelwright, Philip, ed. *The Presocratics*. New York: Odyssey, 1966.

Willey, Basil. *Nineteenth Century Studies*. New York: Harper and Row, 1966.

Winch, Peter, ed. *Studies in the Philosophy of Wittgenstein*. New York: Humanities Press, 1969.

————. "Can We Understand Ourselves?" *Philosophical Investigations* 20 (1997): pp. 195–204.

Wittgenstein, Ludwig. *Blue and Brown Books: Preliminary Studies for the 'Philosophical Investigations'*, second ed. New York: Harper and Row: 1960.

———. *Culture and Value.* Edited by G.H. von Wright, translated by Peter Winch. Chicago: University of Chicago Press, 1980.

———. *Last Writings on the Philosophy of Psychology, Vol. I: Preliminary Studies for Part II of 'Philosophical Investigations,' 1949–1951.* Edited by G.H. von Wright and Heikki Nyman, translated by C.G. Luckhardt and Maximilian A.E. Aue. Chicago: University of Chicago Press, 1982.

———. *Last Writings on the Philosophy of Psychology, Vol. II: The Inner and the Outer, 1949–1951.* Editors and translators as above. Oxford: Blackwell, 1992.

———. *Lectures and Conversations on Aesthetics, Psychology, and Religious Belief.* Student notes edited by Cyril Barrett. Berkeley: University of California Press, 1966.

———. *Wittgenstein's Lectures on the Foundations of Mathematics: Cambridge, 1939.* Student notes edited by Cora Diamond. Ithaca: Cornell University Press, 1976.

———. *Notebooks: 1914–1916,* 2nd ed. Edited by G.H. von Wright and G.E.M. Anscombe, translated by Anscombe. Chicago: University of Chicago Press, 1979.

———. *On Certainty.* Edited by G.E.M. Anscombe and G.H. von Wright, translated by Denis Paul and Anscombe. New York: Harper and Row, 1969.

———. *Philosophical Grammar.* Edited by Rush Rhees, translated by Anthony Kenny. Berkeley: University of California Press, 1974.

———. *Philosophical Occasions: 1912–1951.* Edited by James C. Klagge and Alfred Nordmann. Indianapolis: Hackett, 1993.

———. *Philosophical Investigations,* 3d ed. Translated by G.E.M. Anscombe, edited by Anscombe and Rhees. New York: Macmillan, 1958.

———. *Philosophical Remarks.* Edited by Rush Rhees, translated by Raymond Hargreaves and Roger White. Chicago: University of Chicago Press, 1975.

———. *Remarks on Color.* Edited by G.E.M. Anscombe, translated by Linda L. McAlister and Margarete Schättle. Berkeley: University of California Press, 1977.

———. *Remarks on the Philosophy of Psychology, Vol. I.* Edited by G.E.M. Anscombe and G.H. von Wright, translated by Anscombe. Chicago: University of Chicago Press, 1980.

————. *Remarks on the Philosophy of Psychology, Vol. II.* Edited by G.H. von Wright and Heikki Nyman, translated by C.G. Luckhardt and M.A.E. Aue. Chicago: University of Chicago Press, 1980.

————. *Remarks on the Foundations of Mathematics,* revised ed.. Edited by G.H. von Wright, Rush Rhees, and G.E.M. Anscombe; translated by Anscombe. Cambridge, Mass.: MIT Press, 1978.

————. *Tractatus Logico-Philosophicus.* Translated by D.F. Pears and B.F. McGuinness. New York: The Humanities Press, 1961.

————. *Wittgenstein and the Vienna Circle,* conversations recorded by Friedrich Waismann. Edited by B.F. McGuinness, translated by Joachim Schulte and McGuinness. New York: Harper and Row, 1979.

————. *Wittgenstein's Lectures: Cambridge 1932–1935,* from the notes of Alice Ambrose and Margaret Macdonald. Edited by Alice Ambrose. Totowa, N.J.: Rowman and Littlefield, 1979.

————. *Wittgenstein's Lectures: Cambridge 1930–1932,* from the notes of John King and Desmond Lee. Edited by Desmond Lee. Chicago: University of Chicago Press, 1980.

————. *Wittgenstein's Lectures on Philosophical Psychology, 1946–1947.* Edited from student notes by P.T. Geach. Chicago: University of Chicago Press, 1988.

————. *Zettel.* Edited by G.E.M. Anscombe and G.H. von Wright, translated by Anscombe. Berkeley: University of California Press, 1970.

Index to Sections
in *Philosophical Investigations*

Index